The 10 Secrets of WORSHIP

Emmanuel Christoe

By
Emmanuel Christoe

www.emmanuelchristoe.com

The 10 Secrets of Worship

The 10 Secrets of ® Worship

Copyright © 2017 by Emmanuel Christoe Musasizi
ISBN: 978-9970-9708-1-0: PAPER BACK
Published by Najivunia Publishers
Printed in USA
PAGES: 138 PAGES
SIZE: 5.5 X8.5
www.emmanuelchristoe.com

This book is available at all online book platforms and book stores Worldwide in E-book/Kindle, Audio Product and Paperback.

ABOUT THE AUTHOR

Emmanuel Christoe Musasizi is tremendous international Speaker, a Leadership coach, a Bible teacher, a Church Planter, a counselor, and a Business expert. Emmanuel Christoe Musasizi is the founding president of WATO International Organization.

DEDICATION

I dedicate this book to pastors/ Leaders and to the entire body of Christ Globally. It is such an honor to share this message with everyone reading this book, a message which carries the purpose and the will of God towards us all. For this purpose everything came into existence, and we all live for the Glory of God to be manifested.

True Worship is the center of God's Will, it is the message that surpasses whatever sacrifices that we can offer. The book teaches how truly we can express our worship and also fulfill this purpose in a manner that pleases God.

ACKNOWLEDGMENT

THE HOLY SPIRIT
I acknowledge, my best friend
The Holy Spirit. He means the World to me. He takes a
principal place as my Mentor, Teacher and Revealer.
The Holy Spirit revealed to me the ten secrets of
Worship, the message am sharing with you in this
Volume.
DEAR HOLY SPIRIT YOU ARE MY BEST TEACHER,
MENTOR, MODEL, AND FRIEND EVER!

Dr. BENARD BOGERE SSENKUBUGE

*I acknowledge Dr. BENARD BOGERE SSENKUBUGE.
The president of Keep Left Foundation, the Founding
President   of Uganda Charitable and Benevolent
Teamwork (UCBT). In a time when I was hopeless, filled
with fear, abandoned, rejected and   desperate in life,
Dr. Bernard picked me up and took me in as his own
son.
I learned a lot of lessons and wisdom through
Submitting under him.
Dear Dad.
Everything I am is a product of your mentorship.*

Dr. SELINA RWASHANA

*Special thanks to my prayer partner
Dr. SELINA RWASHANA is a Doctor
of psychiatry, a former Head of Uganda Nursing
Council.
After receiving
an instruction from the Holy Spirit to write this book,
Dr. Serena was the first person to know about this
assignment after sharing it with her. When I shared with
her this idea, being a prayerful woman,   she grabbed
my hand for a word of prayer. In the process of writing
this book, being that it was my first book, I received a lot
of criticism from all angles whom I shared with my
scripts to advise me on how best I could   present my
message in a vibrant articulation.
Dr. Selina encouraged me strongly and also advised me
not to listen to any kind of negativity, and she said to me
these words
"God knew your weakness but still chose you
for this course". "God does not use perfect
People, He uses the foolish of this
World." Dear Dr. Selina,*

May God increase you and your family as well!

Rev. JOHN ZZIWA

Am always thankful to God for being your son, a great Patriarch of God and an incredible bible teacher. You taught me the way of the Lord and for this reason am so proud of myself for the good foundation you gave me. Reveland John Zziwa is my biological Father. He is the Founding President of God's Glory Churches in Uganda, K. Bible College and Jozzi Group of Companies

Pastor. JANET ZZIWA
I also acknowledge my Dearest
Mother Pastor. JANET ZZIWA; you are
always the best mother on my Universe.
Bishop. Janet Zziwa is my biological mother. She is
the overseer of Global Revival Churches in Uganda,
My mother made a great contribution in my early
childhood stage, she imparted in me a seed of ministry,
and for this reason my life has been turned into a person
I am. She always taught me the word of God and also
gave me an opportunity to preach on her platform
wherever she was invited to minister when I was only
9 years young. My mother always treated me as a
servant of
God, and nick named me Pastor Kawuka, which means
the
smallest insect, since I was tiny and dark sickened.
She could always invite me to preach first before
she preached on every platform she stepped on.

She taught me how to address people and how to present
the message. Thank you Jesus for letting me be borne
by her. Am so proud for having been borne by a
Spiritual Mentor like my Mum. I love you Mum.
You are the best gift I have ever received from God!

FAITH MIREMBE
FAITH MIREMBE is my Twin Sister,
she was borne 30 minute after I was born;
My Twin Sister has been my number one   supporter,
Sponsor and Next of kin ever since I joined ministry.
We have fought together, lost together, cried together and
finally won together. She has witnessed my breezing from nothingness to the top. She knows my story, my in and out. She is my best friend and such a gift from God. During the process of writing this book, she was my proof reader, and always encouraged me to push on till I finished the all project of this edition.

PHEOBE MIREMBE
PHOEBE MIREMBE is my Church sister,
a bible Teacher and a Pastor. God has used Phoebe in
the process of bringing this book in writing, Editing and
publication. She offered her computer machines to work
on this project till the book
was finally published. May God richly bless you
Phoebe for the sweet spirit in you!

TABLE OF CONTENTS;

Introduction

A lot of definitions and interpretations have been written about worship by many scholars. It is vivid that true Worship makes a good debatable motion. This edition simply answers almost every question about Worship. In here you will learn the Following:-

What is true worship?

Who is a true worshiper?

What is the place for worship?

Whose is worship?

Why should we worship?

When should we worship?

How should we worship?

What does it take to worship?

Is worship music?

Is worship utterance?

What is worship to God?

What is worship to us?

The story of Jesus with a Samaritan woman begins with Jesus asking for water, and ends at God seeking for true worshipers. This is the book which reveals deeper knowledge about Godliness, thus a study guide of living for the divine purpose.

Chapter 1

GOD AND WORSHIP

ISAIAH 45:5
I am the LORD, and there is no other; apart from me there is no God.

Honor is for positions, respect for dignity, but worship is for God.

MATHEW4:10
"you shall worship the Lord your God, and Him only you shall serve".

Honor in regard to positions is simply acquired thereafter one's prominent achievements and success, as a result of hardworking for recognition in the games of politics, sports, music, entertainment media, as well as in the business arena in order to certify and qualify. This is how it matches with man standards rendering to the natural awareness, but with Godliness it is quite a different concept, in that, God does not need to perform, compete, and contest for his name's sake.

God does not need to bid, wrestle and tussle for his competence, He is highly above every position, power, pre-eminence, recognition and ranks. His greatness and superiority exceeds a minor honor for Him to be tested, examined and nominated for silver and golden medal awards. He is not a human to be voted, elected, weighed and judged for the sake of His reference and dominance. God is extra, supper-qualified to be backed, affirmed and approved by the natural charisma in respect to His beyond compare worthiness and virtue. Many people try to test and examine God's competence and dexterity with their natural wisdom and physical needs, with a sense of making him prove his Godliness by dancing their tune. God's positivity or negativity towards our natural lustful desires is not what proves His supremacy, He was; He is; and He will always be, whether he performs or not. That is to say, God is neither a performer nor an actor but Sovereign. God is surpassingly and superlatively worthy of Glory and adoration through our sincere worship, and for this reason, we ought to worship Him beyond measures, for his greatness and worthiness are incomparable.

Respect

Respect regarding to dignity is solely for mortal men, but Godliness is neither a position, nor a situation, or a circumstance which affects God's superiority for action and reaction. That is to say; God does not need honor or a high respect as for political leaders, heads of departments and nobles who are admired by men for him to feel at place. Considering His invisible personality, Him being a spirit, God does not need natural reputation, neither does he bear a caliber, nor a character of how He should conduct himself or respond towards different situations and circumstances, as anticipated by people regarding to respect. God is not a human, and as we worship, we should express our worship in Spirit.

Worship is respect and submition.

ROMANS 13, respect the authority, everyone must submit to governing authorities.

God is Supreme and an everlasting Ruler over the Universe. He rules over the Earth through Kings and other political leadership settings, for the Earth to be in shape and orderliness. In this manner, we ought to honor and respect our leaders, for their positions and services rendered to us in our respective localities, as we bear in mind that there is no leadership which does not come from God.
As true worshipers, we ought to honor and respect God through submitting under authorities, because God rules in the kingdom of men, and gives it to whoever He wills.

HEBREWS 13:17; have confidence in your Leaders.

The Glory of God.

ISAIAH 42:8, I am the lord that is my name. I will not share my glory with men.

God has shared His honor, respect and authority with kings, rulers, princes and princesses amongst others, but as for worship, He has reserved for His peculiar Glory.

God is a jealousy God, and above Him there is no any other. That is to say, before the universe, galaxies and the biosphere of planet Earth, God was, He is, and He will always be. He is the genesis and the extremity. Meaning, he is the Alpha and Omega; beginning and the end. Since God is for worship and worship is for God, in this we conceive that worship has lived far beyond longevity to genesis, and will always live unceasingly, as long as the everlasting God lives. In this articulation, we perceive that God cannot live without worship, and worship is not worship without God.

JOHN 1:3 All things were made through Him, and without Him nothing was made.

However, nothing can extract the two; God and worship. And this simply means that God without worship is not God but an idle, and worship without God is not worship but idolatry.

EXODUS 32:8 "They have turned aside quickly out of the way which I commanded them. They have made themselves a molded calf, and worshiped it and sacrificed to it, and said,' this is your god, O Israel, that brought you out of the land of Egypt.

In this we grasp that whatever we get obsessed to and even value in reference to God is idolatry. Whenever we spend most of our time busy at our own schedules, attending dinner parties, watching sports, gambling and betting, making outings and shopping without sparing time for God's worship; wherever you are, and whatever you do definitely takes over God's peculiar Glory, hence his worship.

THE GOD HEAD

ROMANS 1:20 For since the creation of the world His invisible attributes are clearly seen, being understood by the things that are made, even His eternal power and Godhead, so that they are without excuse. COLOSSIANS 2:9 For in Him dwells the fullness of the Godhead bodily;

As worshipers, we should not be ignorant about Godhead, but we should get better understanding about the trinity of God, as we understand that this is the sound doctrine.

What is Godhead? The Godhead is simply edified by the three personalities of God. That is to say; God is three in one, meaning, Father, Son and the Holy Spirit. The trinity of the Godhead edified by the Father, Son and the Holy Spirit is what makes Godliness perfect and complete. These three in one live, think and act in unison. This simply means that there's completely nothing that can isolate the trinity of the Godhead, for they work in common just as humans operate in the three dimensions of life. As we humans operate in body, spirit and soul, so does God. A human being is an icon of three entities; body, Spirit and Soul. Every human is three in one. Meaning, body and soul without a spirit is a corpse, a spirit and soul without a body is a demon. A human being should be these three in one in order to operate on this planet Earth and also qualify for natural life.

God formed man in His very own image; body, soul and spirit, meaning, God is three in one. He is a body soul and spirit. Man was created in the real image of God the Father, Son and the Holy Spirit. The three dimensions of humanity represent the three personalities of God the Father, Son and the Holy Spirit.

Man was created in the image of God the father.

JOHN 4:24 God is a spirit.

In here, we should understand that Our Spirits are the true image of God the Father, for He is a spirit.

Man was also created in the image of the Holy Spirit. As worshipers we out to understand that God the Holy-Spirit is the soul hence the mind of the Godhead;

1CORINTHIAN2:11 For who knows a person's thoughts except their own spirit within them? In the same way no one knows the thoughts of God except the Spirit of God.

In this text, as we learn that we are God's very image, here we perceive that our Souls (mind) represent the true image of the Holy Spirit, for he is the mind of God. **Man was also created in the image of Jesus.**
Wow, what an astonishing personality that we bare. How beautiful it sounds for having been created in the image of Jesus. In this acknowledgment, we glimpse on the fact that our physical bodies are the true image of Jesus Christ; God the son

COLOSSIANS1:15 Christ is the visible image of the invisible God. He existed before anything was created and is supreme over all creation.

Our bodies are the true image of God the Son, for he is the body of God. Jesus is the body of the Godhead hence God in the physical form.
Leaning on this understanding as worshipers, the true Christian doctrine and statements of our faith should not be contradictorate to the trinity of the Godhead. We ought to believe in God the Father and the Son whom He gave for our sake, as well as the Holy Spirit. This should also be the similar manner as we gather in the

name of the Father, Son and the Holy Spirit, but not in solitary or believe just in one of them and we neglect the trinity. For it is converse and incompatible to believe just in one of them and we neglect the Trinity of the God Head.

FATHER +SON- HOLY SPIRIT=CULT
FATHER+HOLY SPIRIT-SON=CULT
SON-FATHER-HOLY-SPIRIT=CULT
FATHER+SON+HOLY-SPIRIT=GOD

1JOHN 5:7 For there are three that bear witness in Heaven: the Father, the Word, and the Holy Spirit; and these three are one. MATHEW 3:16,17 When He had been baptized, Jesus came up immediately from the water, and behold, the Heavens were opened to Him, and He saw the Spirit of God descending like a Dove and alighting upon Him. 17: And suddenly a voice came from Heaven, saying," This is my beloved son, in whom I am well pleased.

Relying on the truth of this scripture, the ordinance of the Trinity of Godhead should also be implemented and exploited in our sincere worship for it to emerge worthwhile and complete. Every time we worship, we should always offer our sacrifice in the name of the Father, Son and the Holy Spirit.

Most of us whenever we worship we try to pinpoint each of these three in particular which is reputable and acceptable but not competent. In this orientation, we ought to know that we worship the Father through the son, as well as the son through the Holy Spirit.

Some of us take the Holy Spirit as the least of the Godhead, and others take Him just as a mere helper, guider, friend, fire and power. We should understand that all of these elements are just portraits of His personality, but the Holy Spirit is God. And in this reference, we ought to Worship God through the Holy Spirit, as well as God through the Son Jesus Christ. We should always make mention of his precious name in our worship; for the Holy Spirit is worthy of adoration through our worship.

Chapter 2

WORSHIP IS A PURPOSE

EPHESIANS 3:11 According to the eternal purpose which he purposed in Christ Jesus our Lord:

As I take you through the second chapter of this course of worship, I want to reveal to you a secret about purpose in a very unique approach. Did you know that purpose is the meaning of life, and life defines the truth about Purpose?

Before I take you any further, the following definitions bring about better understanding of what purpose simply means.

According to many common interpretations, Purpose can simply be defined as the goal, intention or reason for which something is created, exists, done, made or used for. All these definitions are true and clear about purpose, and relying onto this revelation, we learn that even creation was a product and blend result of purpose, and without purpose creation would have not taken place.

Did you know that God is a God of purpose that even in every particular move he makes purpose is the platform? Purpose is the origin source and the mother of God's plans as well as creation in general. Here we understand that purpose was the fuel and amplifier for the idea of creation. This also implies that God never created the universe just because of a will, but in here we learn that in every God's plan purpose is the fuel behind each of His particular willfulness, and due to purpose God created everything that we see, love and enjoy. In this revelation we should also consider this important that Man is a product of purpose and without purpose man would have not been created. The idea of creating man was such a brilliant idea which also came up as a result of purpose. And in this sense, as we anticipate man being God's perfect idea, here it clearly reveals that purpose is the mother and the procreator of ideas, plans and significance.

As worshipers we should also take a note that purpose is the most powerful, preeminent and prevailing element on the Universe, in that, the most important and elite mean solar day of your lifetime is the day when you glimpse on the absolute purpose for your existence. Purpose is also viewed as the driver and leadfoot for action and reaction. Purpose can push you forward; awake you early in the morning; make you endure all; with hopefulness and prospect for the bloom ahead of you.

As I take you through this journey of purpose, I want to let you know that purpose is an infancy, yet a starting point for a journey or race. Purpose is also a token thus a guarantee for attainment, achievement and accomplishment. This simply elevates that every attainment, achievement and accomplishment in life has to be amplified by purpose to reach the apex of its course.

If we men act and react towards our common goals and succeed, then at which level can God be limited or hindered to fulfill his transcendent excellent ideal, hence purpose? In this aspect, as we learn that God's purpose is always perfect and surpassing, we should also ask ourselves this question; **what was God's purpose behind the idea of creation?** If there is any optimal-fitting purpose for creation, worship must be the one. Everything that we see, love and enjoy came as a result of worship. That is to say, worship is the mother of creation, and creation is a Shangri-La product of worship.

What was God's optimal purpose for creating planet Earth?

God created the Earth as a training ground for a worshiper. In this realm, each individual person has to taste the reality of this life combat and worldliness before we qualify for eternity. In this course of practicality, there are many tests trials and errors that we experience as part of our physical training docket. Most of these life experiences; trials, tests and challenges drive us so radically even to the ambit of killing our focus from the ideal of life, but we have to fight in order to win. And as we try much as we can to win through this life venture, we should always live with awareness that these worldly desires are just short time know-hows. For example, life is a school of experience where we taste love and loneliness, wealth and poverty, diseases and good health, happiness and sorrow. After we have tasted the flavor of success; learned all the wisdom; achieved lifetime goals; enjoyed love and acceptance; gained status and prominence, here we should always ring a bell that worship is the borderline and the extremity of our destine-edge after this mortal life deal. Therefore, as we bid to fulfill our pure purpose and the real meaning for this natural adventure, we should always cock our minds into true worshipers. In this orientation, we should not put all our premier focus on this short life experience, but always to live as we zoom into our final destination which is the life after times.

As worshipers, we should also strike a note that it is always our task to either pass the life tests in order to befit God's plan behind our creation, or fail and Hell becomes our final destination for eternity.

Worship is the author and the mother of creation. According to GENESIS 1, here you can imagine how God formed the Universe with all the dazzling beauty and elegancy of planet Earth. The magnificent sun and the beauteous moon and the colorful stars in the upper space makes me marvel of His wisdom and artistry. Imagine how God separated the waters from the firmament and the waters gathered in one place according to His word, this makes me wonder of his greatness. The abundance of the living creatures; the birds in the air, the creeping things and the beasts of the field, all He fabricated and fashioned for His worshiper to enjoy and bring Him back all the Glory. Whenever I think about it all, it makes me wonder of how darling worship is to God, and how lovesome a worshiper is to His creator!

For only our sake [worshipers], and for the sake of His treasured worship everything came into existence! What a great mystery!

If creation of man was God's perfect idea, then worship is the mother of ideas, dreams, and visions.

GENESIS 1:26. Then God said, "Let us make man in our own image, according to our likeness.

Have you ever considered the incarnate purpose of your ravished beauty and the fact that you're after God's perfect alikeness? Your fascinating appearance is not meant for occasions and exhibitions, worship is the whole idea behind your beautiful loveliness. In this attribute, we should also understand that glory is the ulterior motive at the heels of our delightful appearance, then your good-looking husband or lovely wife, ultimately.

ISAIAH 43:7. The reason for creation of man was to glorify God and enjoy Him.

As worshipers we should understand that there is no glory without worship. These two of a kind are combo, meaning, worship and glory are coordinates. These two cohabit, hence live together as husband and wife, and can never be separated or parted. That is to say, cease to worship and glory will disappear. But, it is also important to note that there can be worship without Glory, and this simply means that Glory is the bid behind the vim of our worship.

In this perception, we ought to understand that worship is not excitement, exhibition and entertainment but a spiritual act of expression. Worship is not a performance but a purpose. Therefore, any kind of worship without glory is not worship with purpose but worship with gossip.

If in life there's a purpose for existence, there is no a corporeal purpose like worship. We don't live to just exist, and if it was so; there then would have not been a difference between us and the wild beasts, and the trees at the fields. But, even though they have no mind to discern like we humans, just their mere existence and appearance glorifies God.

If men have goals to carry through and bring to pass, there is no a crystalline goal like worship. Worship is like a pursued goal to God. Imagine your beautiful-self since that day you were born, it has been quite a journey. Growing from infantry and teenage to the elderly where you can discern rightly and you finally made up a great lifetime decision when you accepted Jesus as your Lord and savior is such a long journey. Eventually, here and now you're reading the Ten Secrets of Worship and getting acquainted on God's idea behind your creation as a true worshiper who is desirable of Him. If there is a clarion reason for one to live, worship must be the definite one and only.

ISAIAH 38:18, for the dead cannot praise you.

In this text of the context, we zoom that breath is the license, warrant and permit for worship. Every morning you hike from the sleep coma, every birthday you will ever celebrate, every time spent and often wasted, all are guaranteed by the license of breath till the day it finally expires.

Here is a challenging question I impose to you:

As you cerebrate the gift of life, how much has God benefited from the license that He invested in you? It is very important to acknowledge that God can only benefit in every breath that you ever- take through your sincere worship. Worship is the fruit and the synthetic return to God for the breath of life. Imagine, how much money you have spent on your health through medical checkups; buying all kind of medicine and supplements; taking hydrotherapy and be sincere to yourself, if God could only bill you for every breath you have ever taken since you were born without missing even a micro second without oxygen; how could we have afforded for life? Worship is the guarantee for a successful life and life its self is success, yet death is the apex of failure. As

I conclude this second chapter, I make it a point for you always to remember that breath is the license for worship. Man is a product of worship.

Chapter 3

WORSHIP IS A NEED

PHILIPPIANS 4:19
But my God shall supply all your needs according to his riches in glory by Christ Jesus.

In this third chapter of this edition, another secret of worship is revealed. This revelation describes worship as a need.

According to different dictionaries, needs are described in many unique ways. Needs are defined as basic necessities, requirements, essentials, wants, requisites, prerequisites, demands and the desideratum of life. However, in this revelation a need is described as worship, and as we dig deeper into this knowledge, you will get more acquainted on demonstration of true worship through times of need.

Basic necessities are drivers of our day-to-day life physically, spiritually, and emotionally, and in this sensibility there is completely no way that we can make it substantially when our material requisites of life demand beyond provisional supply. This is not the case with only our natural standards of living, but also the same applies to our spiritual demand. And by this philosophy, we perceive that if our spirits are not prudently sustained and maintained perfectly well, it inspires a spiritual relapse and flop. However, needs in regard to demand are natural, regular and consistent. Needs are normal, meaning they contribute much towards life experience. Needs are neutral, implying that we live a balanced animation.

At this point of view, we should note that all living organisms including the micro ones are candidates to needs so long as they live. Needs are everyone's dancing tune, yet a cyclic test of life. In this reference, we cannot live without needs, since needs are part of our lifetime experience.

In this orientation, we learn that if all living organisms rely on needs, how about God himself. Considering the fact that God is a living God, God has needs just as we do. Life revolves around needs, and needs are clear edification for real life. Meaning, you cannot live without needs, yet you cannot need without life.

Concerning needs, there are some biblical examples where Jesus himself was in need and it took a helping hand by the people who were available to meet his needs.

How do we meet God's needs?

JOHN 4:7. A woman of Samaria came to draw water. Jesus said to her, "Give me a drink".

In this story we lecture on how we meet God's needs, and we learn that we meet God's needs by providing to the needy. We meet God's needs through helping the disadvantaged, supporting the down to last cent, feeding the hungry, accommodating strangers, and also taking responsibility of widows and orphans in our societies. Exercising the corporal spiritual works of grace to the needy is the pure and sincere love to God, and it is the complete worship beyond utterance. At this point of view, we cannot claim that we love God and hate man at the same time. Since man was created after God's very own Likeness. In this perception God's love in us is clearly demonstrated through loving each other, just as Christ has loved us. By loving people, we can also draw many to Jesus than just preaching to them without practical deeds of love. The neglected and abandoned persons, and those who are considered as nuisance in our societies are the people we ought to love.

MATHEW 35:25 for I was hungry and you gave me something to eat. I was thirsty, and you gave me a drink. MATHEW 21:3 and if any one says anything to you, you shall say, "the Lord has need of them" and immediately He will send them.

Worship is partnering with God
Here we learn that sincere worship is about partnering with God. In this manner, we partner with God through meeting God's needs pertaining to his work and ministry. Whenever we give our money and material wealth into God's work, we express the sincere worship, ultimately. By doing so, there is no other expression of worship beyond partnership.
Some of us only care about our personal needs, and this is due to our selfish ambitions. As true worshipers, here we learn that we should not be on the receivers' side only, but we should also give generously into God's work without hesitance.

As we bank on God's help for each and everything, can we also be reliable at often times when God is in a desperate need of us? However, if man's physical needs are food, shelter, clothes but to mention a few in order to live, then a question is asked.

Does God also have needs?

And if God would have a need, then what would that need be? What would that thing be that God cannot do or live without?

As we clearly know that God made all that man considers to be needs, we should simply understand that all of the creation was made for man to enjoy, and for this reason they cease to be needs to God. In this reference, even though creation ceases to be needs to God, there is something that God failed to create. There is solitarily one and only surpassing element that God cannot do for Himself, and of which He considers to be the principal want. God has created everything on the Universe, but he cannot worship himself. Worship is God's prime need, necessity, requirement, essential, want, requisite, prerequisite, demand and the desideratum of his life. God cannot do, or even live without worship.

Provision is the answer to needs.

Whenever a need punches the clock, there is always a call for provision. However, provision is not all important without needs.

GENESIS 22:7 But Isaac spoke to Abraham his father and said, "My father!" And he said, here I am, my son." Then he said "look, the fire wood, but where is the lamb for the burnt offering?"

As we humans await and count on God for provision yet our confidence and trust calls upon seeking praying and fasting, the same applies to God. God desperately seeks for someone who can suit, suffice and quench His lead preference, passion and thirst for worship. Meaning, God seeks for a pure genuine worshiper!

GENESIS 22:8 And Abraham said, "My son, God will provide for Himself the lamb for the burnt offering."

In this text, we learn how God tested Abraham when he asked him to give to Him his only son Isaac as a sacrifice. Here Abraham's worship was being tested. Not many of us would be genuine at offering living sacrifices of worship, yet we are very obedient at verbal expression. Here we learn that worship can be given in form of tangible and visible material things, meaning worship is meeting physically tangible needs.

JOHN 4:23 "But the hour is coming, and now is, when the true worshipers will worship the father in spirit and truth; for the father is looking for such to worship Him. According to this new revelation of worship, we understand that worship is not an easy practice and there are a few people who can fulfill the requirement of true worship. There are more singers and speakers in church than loving people, care givers and donors to the poor. We should also understand that God's reliance on us for His truthful worship as a need for His contentment is not just an expression of any form, but we should honestly consider the exact appropriate Spiritual action in truth, which is after His true desired expectations for His supremacy to reign with nothing wanting.

Fruits of true Worship
Whenever a need is not met it results to lack of confidence, insecurity and even loss of life. But, once a need is met, there then one is confident and even lives a life of meaning.

GENESIS 22:10,11, 12, 13, 14. [10]And Abraham stretched out his hand and took the knife to slay his son. [11]But the angel of the Lord called him from Heaven and said, "Abraham, Abraham!" so he said, "Here I am." [12]And he said, "Do not lay your hand on the lad or do anything to him; for now I know that you fear God, since you have not with-held your son, your only son, from me." [13] Then Abraham lifted his eyes and looked, and there behind him was a ram caught in the thicket by its horns. So Abraham went and took the ram, and offered it up for a burnt offering instead of his son. [14]And Abraham called the name of the place, The-LORD-Will provide, as it is said to this day, "In the mount of the LORD it shall be provided."

Since worship is God's surpassing prerequisite, it has to be met for Him to answer our prayers and also cater for our natural desideratum of life as well. Meaning, we ought to meet each other's needs, that is to say, God and man for the good of both of us.

JOHN 4:10 Jesus answered and said to her, "If you knew the gift of God, and who is it who says to you, „Give me a drink", you would have asked Him, and He would have given you living water."

Since God loves us, we ought to love Him more because love which has not been shared is not agape but something else. However, love counting on giving, we ought to give and support others as an expression of our true and pure devotedness to our God.

Worship through giving demonstrates God's love
Love is not optional and falling in love is natural, and to everyone who has been there, I am proven right that

gifts affirm a growing relationship, and expresses one's feelings approximately.

Worship is giving honor and adoration to God.
Worshiping willingly with a full expression of actions like the twenty four elders is the complete and sincere worship, which we ought to learn and adopt in order to offer a competent offering of worship without blemish.

:10,11 the twenty-four elders fall down before Him who sits on the throne and worship Him who lives forever and ever, and cast their crowns before the throne, saying: You are worthy O Lord," To receive glory and honor and power; For You created all things, And by Your will they exist and were created." REVELATION 4:8 The four living creatures, each one having six wings, were full of eyes around and within. And they do not rest day or night, saying: "Holy, Holy, Holy, Lord God almighty, Who was and is and is to come!"

Life revolving around needs and yet worship is a need to the Living God, we should perceive this and also adopt the same behavior of the four living creatures, which ceases not day and night to worship. We should also carry the same principle in our day to day life for God always to count on us for His everlasting Glory. As we meet God's need on a daily basis that is to say worship, it guarantees God's constant and reliable provision to us, as we lean on each other regarding to needs.

PSALMS 37:4 delight yourself in the Lord and He will give you the desires of your Heart.

Chapter4

WORSHIP IS A LIFESTYLE.

The fourth chapter of this codex reveals worship as a simple practice, and it brings this wisdom to a level of normal life, common personalities and appreciating talents. This chapter simply interprets worship as a life style hence a way of living day to day practical experiences.

Lifestyle simply refers to various ways of living by different people, depending on characteristics, contrasts, changes, inequalities and differences in culture, localities, attitudes, desires and choices. This definition simply edifies life as worship, and it defines every human as a worshiper regardless of each person's uniqueness.

God formed man in His own likeness, and with perfection and wisdom man was formed, that there was absolutely nothing wanting and missing. We were wonderfully, perfectly and gloriously made, for God is AL perfect.

GENESIS 1:26. Then God said, "let us make man in our own image, according to our own likeness".

God is surpassingly beautiful beyond description, for who are we to be made after His own alikeness! God's image, beauty and glory is utterly revealed in man, and for one to be acquainted on God's perfection in beauty and loveliness should just take a good look at oneself in a mirror. Meaning, your beautiful appearance and handsomeness was God's perfect idea.

JESUS IS BOTH GOD AND MAN.

MARK 14:62 Jesus said, "I am. And you will see the son of man sitting at the right hand of the power, and coming with the clouds of Heaven".

As we clearly review this scripture, more evidence is revealed here that Jesus is 100% man yet God.

REVELATION 1:13 And in the midst of the seven lamp stands One like the son of man, clothed with the garment down to the feet.
REVELATION 14:14 Then I looked, and behold, a white cloud, and on the cloud sat One like the son of man.

This scripture definitely confirms Jesus's true iconic identity as a person.
As we go through this chapter, a lot of wisdom is revealed even about heavenly beings and angels.
Did you know the truth about Angels?
The angels were not formed in God's complete likeness, but were also created in a beauteous kind of artistry for the glory of God. In this conduct, it may sound a bit perplexing in one's hearing, and in this certainty I make it a point that there is no one or even any creation

including the Heaven itself that was created or lived before the image of God. The image of God has lived before Adam, and as long as God lives, so will it.

REVELATION 1:8 I am the alpha and the Omega, the beginning and the end," "who is and who was and who is to come the Almighty."

MAN IS GREATER THAN THE ANGELS.
In this lecture you will discover that man exceeds the angels. This is so due to man having been formed after God's own complete image with the three complete personalities of God, body, spirit and mind. The Angels in Heaven don't possess God's full image, simply because they don't live in the three complete entities, body, spirit and soul.

GENESIS 3:22; And the Lord God said, Behold, the man has become as one of us, to know good and evil: and now, lest he put forth his hand, and take also of the tree of life, and eat, and live forever.

In this scripture, God clarifies how man had become like one of the three identities of the trinity, that is to say, Jesus is God in the physical form. Before the fall of man, Adam was not yet a complete image of God. But, after tasting the tree of knowledge, then he became a mortal god and possessed the image of God the son (JESUS).

MAN EXCEEDS EVEN THE FOUR LIVING CREATURES.

The four living creatures were not created in God's complete image; body spirit and soul. The four living creatures possess only the two identities of God; spirit and mind, but there physical appearance totally differs from God's very physical nature.

REVELATION 4:7 The first living creature was like a lion, the second living creature was like a calf, the third living creature had a face like a man, and a fourth living creature was like a flying eagle.

GOD HAS EXALTED MAN ABOVE THE ANGELS.

HEBREWS 1:5 For to which of the Angels did He ever say: "you are my Son, today I have begotten you"? And again: "I will be to him a Father, and He will be to me a Son"? 6: But when He brings the first born in to the World, He says: "Let all the angels of God worship Him." JOHN 1:12 for as many had received Him, to them He gave the right to become children of God, to those who believe in His name. In this scripture, we hint on the clearance that having been made sons and daughters of God through Christ Jesus, we now possess the true son-ship rights to be called sons and daughters of God. And, as true sons and daughters, we qualify to inherit all God's blessings and promises to Abraham's seed. As Jesus was exalted, we were exalted through Him since we are the body of Christ.

ROMANS 6:8 Now if we died with Christ, we believe that we shall also live with Him. 2 TIMOTHY 2:11-12 This is a faithful saying: For if we died with Him, we shall also live with Him.12: If we endure, we shall also reign with Him.

Angels are servants and attendants to God. And, as we possess the rights of son-ship to God, we definitely qualify for their services as well. In this sense, we understand that God has exalted man even above the angels.

HEBREWS 1:14 Are the angels all not ministering spirits sent forth to minister for those who will inherit salvation?

It is also important to note that the Lord is a God of variety, and that is why in His art of creation He considerably created us differently but the same. We were created different in color, language, cultures, traditions, desires, attitudes and choices as well. Being created with diversities was purposed to fulfill God's will in regard to worship, that which we express in unique forms and styles according to our distinctive uniquenesses.

God enjoys every style of worship, meaning that every one of us in the way we were made was just as a perfect idea to God. For this reason, we don't need to change our appearance or color in order to look like others. We were perfectly and wonderfully made, and God knows each one of us by name. God is well pleased just in the unique ways that He formed us, irrevocably. And in this case we should learn that since worship is after glory, one should not strive to look more radiant in pursuance of exceeding others as long as God's Glory is manifested in you. There are so many beautiful people in the World who abuse and misuse their gorgeous looks by doing pornography and prostitution. But, you should always thank God if your body is still the Centre of His Glory.

CULTURE

In this study, while we ascertain worship as a lifestyle, here we glimpse on how Culture demonstrates people's uniquenesses of their daily living. In this manner, Culture can be defined as art and other manifestations of human intellectual achievements, regarded, collectively. Culture can also refer to characteristics and knowledge of a particular group of people, defined by everything; language, religion, cuisine, social habits, music and arts. But, it can also be viewed as shared patterns of behaviors and interactions, cognitive constructs and understanding which are learned by socialization.

As we sensitively revise on how worship relies much on culture, we understand that if culture is not sensitively examined, it can be a stumbling block to worship as a life style. Culture being a character and knowledge that is defined by religion and social habits, for someone to change from his childhood behaviors and start living a life that glorifies God might not be an easy advancement, since most people cling so hardly on their past experiences. In this sense, the transformation mechanism can quietly not be an easy process to discern, because most people live by their accustomed beliefs, whether right or wrong.

MATHEW 9:16, 17 "No one puts on a piece of unshrunk cloth on an old garment; for the patch pulls away from the garment, and the tear is made worse. 17."Nor do they put new wine into old wine skins, or else the wine skins break, the wine is spilled, and the wine skins are ruined. But they put new wine in the new wine skins and both are preserved.

This context simply edifies that, in order to adopt a new God's culture, we ought to deny ourselves from the past interactions and understanding for us to acquire a Godly desirable character that is to say; a glorious life style as true worshipers.

According to the traditions of the Hebrews, in their theorem women were not viewed as important as men. Women were always left behind even in the spiritual matters of worship. For example, women ordination for priesthood was totally unacceptable, as women were regarded impure to serve as priests. In the Hebrew culture, there was a total discrimination of women, even in their sitting manner at the gatherings women used to be separated from men. In the present day Christian community, we ought to understand that differences in culture are not meant to bring racism and divisions amongst us, rather are to demonstrate uniquenesses in talents and art for better presentation of our worship to God. We also understand that through the blood of the covenant of Christ, we were all sanctified and made as one. In this respect, both men and women are one, irrespective of gender differences.

JOEL 2:29 And also on My men servants and on My maidservants, I will pour out My Spirit in those days. 1 CORINTHIANS 3:9 For we are God's fellow workers; you are God's field, you are God's building.

The differences that we possess in customs, according to each man's origin, or race should not be the platform for disputes amongst ourselves. Here we learn that whenever we breeze into God's presence for worship as Christians, we should always gather in unison as a people in one accord.

ACTS 11:2, 3 and when Peter came up to Jerusalem, those of the circumcised contended with him, 3 saying, "you went into the uncircumcised and ate with them!"

Through the blood of Jesus, we have been sanctified and made as one. We are brothers and sisters through this blood of the covenant, whether Jews or gentiles, circumcised or uncircumcised. Christ has paid such an unimaginable price, just to make us one body and acceptable before God. In this manner, we ought to recognize, understand, appreciate and celebrate the passion of Christ at the cross, every single day of our times.

GALATIANS 3:28 There is neither a Jew nor Greek, there is neither slave nor free, there is neither male or female; for you are all one in Christ Jesus. 29. And if you are Christ's, then you are Abraham's seed and Heirs according to the promises. EPHESIANS 5:1; therefore be imitators of God as beloved children.

Despite the fact that God is a God of variety, we ought not to adopt omnifarious worldly cultures, with senseless marbles and feeling of imperfection in the way we do it [worship]. We should not pop to do our worship in a defying secular form, however modernistic and stylish it might suitably sound according to the worldly frame. Likewise, we should understand that the physical nature hence the worldly system models the church in quite various fashions. That is to say, the world mentors the church in family matters, relationships and networking, planning and developmental activities, academics and church business. The success in the secular world sphere inspires the body of Christ to dream big, pursue dreams, and fulfill the purpose. In this aspect, the church has no reasonable excuse for failure, since we attain the supernatural charisma which is even far beyond the worldly system. Therefore, we should understand that we as Christians, we learn a whole lot from the world system. *JOHN 3:12 I have spoken to you of earthly things and you do not believe; how then will you believe if I speak of heavenly-things?*

While we acknowledge the World order as a role model for the church, in this articulation we should always strike a note that the world being our role model isn't a guarantee for the church to adopt all kind of tones. We should note that mentorship is not all about learning poor characters; adopting weaknesses of your mentor. Mentorship is not about acquiring one's personalities, meaning, the accent and the dressing code. In this aspect, we should also understand that being imitators of Christ doesn't necessarily elevate that one should be a male figure in order to reflect the real image of Christlikeness, for Him having been manifested to us in a male bodily form. In here, we understand that you don't have to become a duplicate of your teacher, rather, develop in to a better teacher.

The Lord led the children of Israel to the land of Egypt with a sure goal of making them as great as Egypt, but not a carbon copy to Egypt. This is the same applies to the church, the church was sent into the world not to simply become equivalent and identical to the worldly methodology, practices and complex. Rather, the church is in the world to learn, be tested, mature and be perfected for the Kingdom of God, meaning, the World is like a training ground. The World is a school.

Concerning mentorship as a process, we should understand that as the world's mentors the church, it isn't a platform for the church to turn into the world's exhibition Centre. For example, being transferred from the most terrible La Sabaneta Prison of Venezuela to the most luxurious Bastoy Prison of Norway is not freedom, but a solution for overcrowding in the prison. This simply means that getting saved is not being born again. Being born again is far beyond a mere confession. At this point of view, you find many people who come to church and still carry on their old life styles of the sinful nature. Here we must understand that Satan is not afraid of your confession and Christianity, but a decided and transformed person causes him headache. Attending church services and still live the old life has no difference between a home detention and prison custody, as long as the Devil can still have access to drive your life perversely. Here we learn that it is not just a matter of being a Christian, but it's more of being transformed and also living a Christ-like portrait.

As we learn more about culture, we must get to know that Lifestyle being a form of worship shouldn't be just of any fashion for the sake of living a Godly glorious entity. And since worship is after glory, any style around the world which abuses the rightful nature of humanity according to the archetype sequence of God should be abolished out of the church, for the sake of God's everlasting glory. For example, there are so many worldly styles of music and dances which have been taken on and adopted by the church, with intent of attracting young people through entertainment, as a hook to draw many to the church. This idea is very excellent, but cannot be reliable. In this case, we should consider a point that in every manner we ought to please God, but not men. God is well aware of the seductive Worldly schemes that we ought to endure and overcome, yet all in all He doesn't expect us to be as perfect, splendid and immaculate as angels in Heaven regarding to our expression of worship. It is always pleasant to God, the way we express our worship in our local form of countenance. God enjoys us the way we are. Culture and differences in customs and beliefs should definitely be over-viewed in worship as a lifestyle.

JAMES 4:4 You adulterous people, don't you know that friendship with the world means enmity with God? 1 JOHN 2:15-17 Do not love this world nor the things it offers to you, for when you love the world, you do not have the love of the Father in you. For the world offers only the craving for physical pleasure, craving for everything we see, and pride in our achievements and possessions. These are not from the Father, but are from this world. And this world is fading away, as long as the things that people crave.

In East Africa, where I was born a Ugandan, before the explorers came and even before colonialists took over, the Arabs were the first foreigners to step in the land of East Africa. There sole interest was trading, as they dealt in slave trading through barter trade. Slave traders took advantage of Africans' ignorance and illiteracy and manipulated our ancestors. This Foreigners bought slaves and ivory in exchange of valueless and cheap items like mirrors. As time went on, some Arabs chose

East Africa to be their permanent place of residence, after they had tasted the beauty of the land to be home. They also intermarried with East African tribes, and eventually a new culture of mixed blood people who are currently known as African Arabs was finally formed. And, as a result of mixed languages, that is to say, Arabic and African local tongues, a new language known as Swahili was ultimately born, which later on became the most popular and finally launched as the official language of the Five East African countries; Uganda, Kenya, Tanzania, South Sudan, Rwanda and Burundi.

At this point of view, it is a wakeup call to church Leaders always to be aware of the worldly system which is intended by the enemy to contaminate the church. Whenever the church intermarries with the worldly system, it simply ends up adopting another culture and even abandoning the true origin that we acquired by faith through Christ Jesus. Whenever the church contaminates the truth with deceit, it eventually creates fake doctrines, divisions and useless sects, amongst the body. The fear of the Lord departs completely, as the world takes over the church, and Grace is misused as people carry on whatever pleases them just like in the days of the Judges when Israel forsook God. Then the church finally ends up in a pathetic state without difference between believers and nonbelievers.

Therefore, the church should always stand firm and strong, not to be taken by every wind and waves but to stick on truth, that's when we shall be able to offer a complete worship without blemish. At this point of view, worship as a life style should advance from just being an act, and turn into a culture, hence a life style.

While the children of Israel lived in a foreign land for over 430 years, for the four generations of their suffering in Egypt never did they adopt the Egyptian culture, neither did their children learn the behaviors of the Egyptian children. The Hebrews believed in their customs, and they never turned away from the God of their ancestors to the gods of the foreign land. This is a standard model picture that the church should adopt to fulfill the purpose of God.

The following scriptures are a guide for you to revise more about this subtopic.

MATHEW 5:13 "you are the salt of the Earth. But if the salt loses its saltiness, how can it be made salty again? JOHN 18:36Jesus said, "My kingdom is not of this world. If it were, my servants would fight to prevent my arrest by the Jewish Leaders.

PHILIPPIANS 3:20But our citizenship is in Heaven. And we await Savior from there, the Lord Jesus Christ.

MATHEW 16:26 What good will it be for someone to gain the world, yet forfeit their soul? Or what can anyone give in exchange for their soul.

2 CORINTHIANS 6:14 Do not be yoked together with the unbelievers.

LOCATION

Location determines people's day to day living, meaning location matters a whole lot concerning life standards.

 King Solomon the preacher, emphasized on time for everything in his codex of the book of Ecclesiastes3, and he noted that to everything there is a season, a time for every purpose under heaven. In this topic, Place for every purpose on the Earth is the focal point.

One of the most important lessons we ought to cover in this subtopic is that, there's absolutely nothing that works out rightly, sidewise its designated premises. That is to say; Hospitals are for the sick; Garages are for vehicle repairs. In this quotation, you cannot seek for medical consultancy from a mechanic engineer, and it is awkward to seek motor servicing from a surgery theater. Here we learn that every place has been designed for specific duties and special operations.

There's always a place for being born, and a place for death. This simply means that life is a transition, people don't usually drown from where they sprung. Your starting spot might not be your end point. Chicago might have been your breezing joint, and Hawaii becomes your destined abode. The same applies to Jesus, he was born in Bethlehem, hidden in Egypt, raised in Nazareth and died in Golgotha. Joseph shifted from Potiphar's house to Prison, and finally to the Palace. It is only the law of cultivation and farming which doesn't corroborate with changes in location. According to the law of cultivation, the place for sowing is the same place for harvesting, even though the seasons for planting and reaping differs accordingly. Here we learn that you cannot expect profits and privileges from where you never invested.

However, in life there are always places for weeping and places for cerebrations. Meaning, it is lunatic to dance at a funeral and then mourn at a dinner party. Lifestyles are determined by location. Lifestyles differ as per each distinctive location, just like changes in weather and seasons, people's ways of living change once they reallocate to new vicinities. New encounters with distinctive people and interactions usually result to changes in behaviors, attitudes, characters, principles, hence advancement in styles of living.

This is the same applies to Worship, worship is a lifestyle. Worship is a behavior, an attitude, character, and a principle. In this sense, we understand that behaving uprightly, and attaining a Godly thinking, developing a Christ-like character and living a spiritually principled life is the true worship, beyond utterance.

By the reference of worship being a lifestyle, differences in locations can simply determine a style of worship. This simply means that people will always do their worship according to their home setting. For example, in the modernistic world, people do their worship according to their stylish way of setting, and this is where power addressing systems are commonly used. At this point of view, we learn that there is a lot much difference between the civilized world and the non-modernized way of setting, regarding to worship as a life style.

According to the local tenor, in the third world African countries, traditional musical instruments are commonly used as the musical accompaniment for worship. However, the modernistic setting is more standardized than the traditional framework, yet God is after Glory, and delights in us all, both modish and locale.

Locations are opted by altitude, yet altitude also determines the weather. Dressing codes keep on changing depending on weather changes of each distinctive place, where you find that some dressing code appears to be indecent to some cultures. This results to criticism amongst the fellow Christians, as everyone tries to be proven right regarding moral ethics of the church. For example, women in the Karamojong region of Northern Uganda don't cover up their breasts, they only cover the lower parts of their bodies and live the upper ones openly uncovered.

Location often times affects worship as a life style, since every place has gotten its own people with different cultures, beliefs and hobbies.

According to Jews, Jerusalem was the place for worship. Every Israelite from all over the world could go to Jerusalem for worship and also to celebrate the Passover feast annually, in remembrance of the day that the Lord brought them from the land of Egypt. But, after the death of King Solomon, Israel split into two and there was Judah as one group in Jerusalem as their capital under King Rehoboam, and then the rest of the 10 tribes of Israel went under Jeroboam in Samaria as their capital.

1 KINGS 12:26 Jeroboam said in his heart that, "now the Kingdom may return to the house of David; If people go up to offer sacrifices to the Lord in Jerusalem, then the hearts of these people will turn back to their Lord, Rehoboam King of Judah." Therefore the king asked advise, and made two calves of gold, and said to the people, "It is too much for you to go up to Jerusalem. Here are your gods, O Israel that brought you out of Egypt!"

In this context, we learn that Jeroboam trans-located worship ceremonies from Jerusalem to Samaria in order to hinder people from going up to Jerusalem for worship for the sake of preserving his kingdom. But, even though he acted in this conduct, still God and the covenant box remained in Jerusalem. As if it was not enough, Jeroboam made a golden calf in reference to the God of Israel, and he even appointed priests who were not Levites to serve and sacrifice to the golden calves, as it was in the Israel custom, regarding to worship. In this matter of contention, we grasp that it is not all about the place; it is all about you; a worshiper's heart! With or without Jerusalem people could still worship, and were even able to make their own image gods, and continued to worship still.

We should understand that God's heart is after a worshiper's heart, but not place. However, God's omnipresence is not all about physical locations or places, but our physical bodies and hearts are the true temples where God dwells.
God's presence hence glory dwells among people but not in physical vicinities. This simply means that whenever we gather in a place for worship, God also

dwells in our midst, and whenever we disperse from our usual places of gathering, God also departs along with us. Therefore, we should understand that it is always our presence that makes God present. The bible affirms it clearly;

PSALMS 137:7-12 7; Where can I go from Your Spirit? Or where can I flee from your presence? 8; If I ascend into heaven, you are there; If I make my bed in hell, behold, you are there. 9; If I take the wings of the morning, and dwell in the uttermost parts of the sea. 10; Even there Your hand shall lead me, and Your right hand shall hold me.11; If I say, "Surely the darkness shall fall on me," Even the night shall be light before me.12; Indeed, the darkness shall not hide from You, But the night shines as the day; The darkness and the light are both alike to You.

This scripture doesn't necessarily elevate that God's presence is everywhere, rather, a pure clearance that there's completely no way that we can sneak away from God's omnipresence, because wherever we dash to, there He goes along with us. In this sense of perception, we should not seek for God's presence, but should be spiritually sensitive as we feel it, and also abide by it, as well as it in us. And, as we live in his presence, we understand that just as the waters fill the sea and the due in the morning covers the space, so does Gods presence also fill the Earth as people also dwell and live on this wonderful bio-globe. In this manner, we perceive that we are carriers of God's presence, and the presence of God dwells within us.

Jerusalem was the place for worship according to the first covenant that God made with the children of Israel, but according to the new covenant through Jesus Christ, we became seeds of Abraham not by blood, but through faith in Christ Jesus. And since we are born of the Spirit but not by will of man, we no longer need to go to Jerusalem for worship. This doesn't necessarily mean that we should not consider places as relevant in regard to worship. But, since we are sons of Abraham through faith, then Jerusalem has also turned into a Spiritual vacancy of worship.

Time has finally come to pass, when true worshipers will worship God from neither Jerusalem nor Samaria, but in Spirit and truth. And since we are the temples for God's dwelling, we ought to know that we are the place for worship, but not the physical vicinities or church auditoriums and pews. Out of our hearts there comes the sincere and true worship, which matches God's desire. At this outlook, we should focus more on building our spiritual temples, than the physical fancy classy beauteous superstructures. In this reference, we should understand that God does not dwell in the temples made by human hands but in hearts.

THE STATE OF HEART

It is the state of your heart which determines the kind of a god, but neither the altar nor the sacrifice. God is so holy, and for this reason, we ought to clean our hearts for God to have room and dwell inside of us. In this sensation, we should note that there is no an empty house. If a person is not Spirit filled, then he is demon possessed; there's no a vacant heart. Meaning, it is the state of your heart which edifies whether it is Jehovah God or an image, since worship without God is idolatry, and God without worship is an image.

God is a Spirit, and for this reason, in Spirit should be our place for worship. If one worships from elsewhere but not in Spirit, then one needs to vacate the premises and relocate for a spiritual vacancy.

PSALMS 91:1 He who dwells in the secret place of the Most High shall abide under the shadow of the Almighty.

I have noticed how most Christians humble themselves in the physical places of worship. Most Christians know how well they can act at church premises because they know that God is always there. So; they respect much the worship auditoriums, and misbehave away from church, little knowing that God dwells among them. Choosing the presence of God as a secret place for your dwelling is the best decision you can ever make for your entire life. It is only in Spirit, where we abide by the shadow of the Almighty. For there is no a lifestyle that we should cherish compared to living in Spirit, and by the Spirit of the Living God.

SEASON

Seasons contribute a whole lot on how people live their lives. People's Lifestyles reflect much on how seasons differ or change accordingly.

GENESIS 8:22 "While the Earth remains, seed time and harvest, cold and heat, winter and summer, and day and night shall not cease.

As we tackle on season in this tract, I just want you to take a second and think about this, "there are no negotiations about seasons; we just have to comply with them". Everything on Earth is forced, ruled, dominated, regulated, directed, supervised, controlled and revolves around seasons. And in this reference, there's absolutely nothing under the sun which is out of control. Our downing in the night and our awakening in the morning every single day; all the work we do; every dream and vision in life; our success and failure, all governed and managed by seasons. Seasons are drivers, rulers and controllers over the Earth. That is to say, Day and night; Times after times; Years after years; Decades after decades; Centuries after centuries; as well as Millennium after millenniums.

The sun and the moon have been appointed by God as signs for seasons, and as long as seasons live, so will they! The Sun has and will always rule over the day, as well as the Moon over the night.

GENESIS 1:16 Then God made greater two lights: the greater light to rule over the day, and the lesser light to rule the night. PSALMS 104:19 He appointed the moon for season: the sun knows it's going down.

Seasons determine our working schedules, and also decide our where, when, and what to do. Therefore, there is no compromise, and every successful business person in the business arena has learnt how to operate and hit his targets by letting seasons determine, direct and decide for him.

GALATIANS 6:9 and let us not grow weary in well doing: for in due season we shall reap, if we faint not.

Fruitfulness and downfall abide by the law of season. Seasons decide everyone's timing for birth, as well as drowning. In this case, it is a complication for one to be born before or passed time, and every premature death is an accident.

ECCLESIASTES 3:1- To everything there is a season, a time for every purpose under the Heaven: 2. A time to be born, and a time to die.

Kings and rulers rise and fall; they come and go according to God's plan as He appoints them for leadership with purpose. Kingdoms over kingdoms pass away, but season is the ruler who never ceases as long the Earth exists.

DANIEL 2:21-And he changeth the time and the seasons: he removeth kings and setteth up kings: he giveth wisdom unto the wise and Knowledge to them who know understanding.

WORSHIP IS ABOVE SEASONS.

Did you know that even though seasons rule over the Earth and also have control over every work of man under the sun, seasons have no power and control over worship? Wow, what an understanding, for it is only and entirely worship which is out of control. **God has exalted His worship even above seasons, and this is ultimately due to His everlasting Glory.** How does it sound in your hearing just to deem how Heaven operates out of seasons? It may sound unreasonably awkward but yet true about the Heavenly wonderland.

In Heaven, there is neither day nor night. In Heaven, there is no any scorching by the sun and moon. In

Heaven, there are no days, weeks, months, years, centuries, and millenniums, due to the fact that there the sun and the moon exists not. Imagine a place where seasons don't change. A place where there is neither winter nor rain; a place where summer and drought don't exist. Heaven was designed in such uniqueness, far beyond the Earthly experience. God the everlasting dwells in such an extra-supper colossal empyrean. Heaven is such a beauteous experience, beyond fantasy. It is a place where they neither sleep nor tire; where sickness, calamity, problems and death exists not, but ever a busy place where angels work day and night, without seasons and weather hindrances.

Since Heaven is neither affected by time nor controlled by seasons, there worship is ceaseless due to an Everlasting Father who never slumbers from generations to generations. His Glory is also everlasting due to the uncontrollable stead relentless worship by the Heavenly hosts. For as long as God lives, there is no limit for worship, hence Glory is perpetual.

REVELATION 4:8 The four living creatures, each one having six wings, were full of eyes around and within. And they do not rest day or night, saying: "Holy, Holy, Holy, Lord God almighty, who was and is and is to come!"

As we ascertain how Heaven is out of seasons, and yet worship is unceasingly constant, in this manner, we ought not to let seasons discern for us on how, why and when should we worship our God. There should totally be nothing, whether circumstances or calamities that should hinder our worship as a lifestyle. For we ought to worship at all times; meaning in good and bad; plenty and drought; cheer and sadness; worship should advance from just being a purpose and turn into one's way of living hence a lifestyle.

JOB 1:20 Then Job arose, tore his robe, and shaved his head; and he fell to the ground and worshiped.

In this scripture, we learn how Job responded in his darkest hour. Indeed Job was such a righteous man before God, and his righteous living was finally approved by the way he responded towards the terrifying moments in his horrible season of tests that he endured. And through it all, Job never denounced his God, regardless of all the pain that he went through. Imagine, if you were the one after losing all the possession; the seven thousand sheep, the three thousand camels, the five hundred yoke of oxen, the five hundred female donkeys, the seven sons and three beautiful daughters; all gone in a scrimp moment. That was the worst omen of all the bad experiences I have ever heard and read about in my entire life. It is so amazing that even in the midst of this calamity; Job could still bow down and worship God! Surely, there is no man who has ever been tested and tried as Job, and his worship was still affirmed true and sincere. Job portrayed such sincere tried and true worship, beyond vignette.

Here a question is asked; are you a worshiper? And if the answer is yes, then how, why, and when do you often worship, with a true and sincere mind? I have noticed how most people can worship throughout the good times and turn into blasphemers by the tune of dryness in their lives. We should genuinely worship at all times.

FRUITS REGARDING TO SEASONS

ISAIAH 55:10-11 For as rain cometh down, and the snow from Heaven, and returneth not thither, but waterth the Earth, and maketh it bring forth the bud, that it may give seed to the sower, and bread to the eater.

In crop farming, we see how seasons determine the planting and the harvesting process. But when it comes to the fruitage and finally to the harvesting time for the repercussions of the produce of one's labor, there seasons can't determinate the quality and the quantity of the harvests. However much it rains or shines, the effort invested always determine the fruitage and the gatherings. As that is the order with natural standard, we must consider this as well as we focus on the spiritual as our focal point. The spiritual seeding and harvesting is neither defined nor edified by time in regard to season. Spiritual sowers plant in seasons and out of seasons, the same insinuating to their reaping process in the harvesting seasons and out of time, due to the impercievable fruitage seasons of their vintage. MATHEW 21:18-46 teaches us to bear fruits in seasons and out of seasons. In this view, we perceive that our worship should not be seasonal.

Here we learn that we ought to be fruitful throughout the year due to the fact that worship is a fruit of the Spirit.

MARK 11:12-14 [12] Now the next day when they had come out of Bethany, He was hungry. [13] And seeing from afar a fig tree having leaves, He went to see if perhaps He would find something on it. When He came to it, He found nothing but leaves, for it was not the season for figs. [14] In response Jesus said to it, "Let no one eat fruit from you again." And His disciples heard it.

In this concept of worship, the Lord doesn't expect us in comparison with the figs. The figs bear only in seasons, and are fruitless out of season. For example, if love and patience are part of the nine fruits of the spirit, then how could we differ from hypocrites if we only love those who love us and deserving? The same should apply to patience which is constructive. We should not be patient only with the bearable circumstances, but even also the intolerable prospects deserve unreserved complete and comprehensive patience. Even though the fig was one of a kind that retained itself with an excuse for having been out of season for fruitage, Jesus' spirit could still diagnose its complications of barrenness. Most of us always give excuses to defend our fruitlessness.

We give such excuses like;
I don't have enough to share with others.
I can't help because I also need help.
I can't risk.
I can't take in an alien, he may harm me.
I have to think about it before I make a final decision.
I have to be wise and careful.
I have to first investigate on this.
I have to balance my books first.
I have to get my partner's consent towards this.
It is none of my business.
I also went through the same and no one cared.
That is life.

To be fruitful simply means:
To give and share what is not enough with others.
To help when you need help as well.

To risk for others.
To lodge a stranger.
To give and help without question.
Giving and offering help does not need you to be of IQ.
You don't need to investigate the one you are helping.
You don't have to be rich to give, rather, requires a big heart.
You can still give even when your partner is not willing.
To Support ideas developed by others.
Whatever you went through was because you had no one to help, now you can help others.
Life is not about selfishness, life is about sharing.

JOHN 15:2 "Every branch in Me that does not bear fruit He takes away, and every branch that bears fruit He prunes, that it may bear more fruit.

Fruitfulness is not all about bearing any, but good ones are the most desirable of God as a result our good statuses.
It is about giving the best; loving with sincerity; purity in heart, truthfulness.
This implies that sincere worship is a product of a pure heart.

MATHEW 7:17-20 [17] "Even so, every good tree bears good fruit, but a bad tree bears bad fruit." [18] "A good tree cannot bear bad fruit, nor can a bad tree bear good fruit. " [19] "Every tree that does not bear good fruit is cut down and thrown into the fire." [20] "Therefore by their fruits you will know them."

This scripture reveals worship as not only a good time frequency, but should always be expressed even when things turn up negative in our lives. A man is like a seed, which is planted, watered and expected to bring forth good fruits by the cultivator. In this we grasp that love being a gift, how can we demonstrate our love to God without action? Worship is a fruit of love, yet true love is about giving.

ATTITUDE

Worship as a lifestyle counts much on people's attitude. People's opinions, understanding, selections, determinations and decisions of how to live their lives count much on their distinct attitude, as the midpoint for their actions and reactions. Attitude sums how one handles, encounters, confronts and resists hazards, catastrophe, hard-knocks and tough-breaks which strike our daily living. Actions and reactions are reflections of attitude, and since worship is a lifestyle, a person's attitude contributes much towards its vigor. In this case, worship comes from a commendatory pure mind; worship is determined by a pure and congruous attitude.

1CORINTHIANS 2:16, for who has known the mind of God that he may instruct Him, HEBREWS 8:10, I will put my laws in their minds. COLLOSIANS 3:2. Set your mind on things above, not on things on the earth.

Worship comes from sterling and sound intellects. In this sense, we learn that people with instinct act with better understanding which results to perfect worship.

It is also relevant to acknowledge that success is a mindset but not a coincidence. Better life starts with better brains. People with poor conception always fail in life. God's will is for us to live a better life of success which brings glory to Him, meaning, You living gloriously starts now, and there then in the eternity after this life. Everything starts with the mindset, then faith next, and finally an expression of true worship result. How well do you think about oneself, and in which perspective do you view and value your life before others do? Every prayer, willingness and yenning in your life can passably come to pass, the same applies to the bad wishes, poor prospects and fears. In this respect, we should adopt a discipline of thinking proficiently good about ourselves and others as well.

Imagine how great dreamers in the world develop such excellent ideas which put them at the topmost and make them multi billionaires. Every prime good thing that we see and admire, all the great achievements which blow our minds, all were once dreams which resulted from a gratifying and good attitude. In this sense, I urge you to have better attitude for better results.

Your challenge is neither your place of work, products, system of service, nor your business partners, your failure intellectually relates to your negative attitude. Many people around the Globe die before their time, due to pressure and heartaches resulting from fearfulness and anxieties of what might happen to them, even without assurance. Fear kills faster than poison, yet most of our fears build from within our brains and poor imaginations.

One day I was at my home with my buddies, and as you know how common and numerous rats are in some poor homes that even cats cannot easily consume them all, there was a rat in my sofa that was scrubbing and interrupting. Then one of my friends suggested that if we could block every passage and force it out of the sofa, it would be easy for us to strike it dead. It was quite a good idea and I was positive, but as we forced it out of the sofa, it started running towards its usual passages, and funny enough; everywhere was perfectly blocked. As this poor rat lost all the hope for life after noticing that it had no way for escape, It finally stopped running, and stood in one place, as it screamed so loudly, hopelessly waiting to die. At the moment I could read its mind how it felt like an already finished poor rat. We instead felt pity for it, yet we finally killed it, of course.

Through this funny incident; I learnt quite a big lesson of how most people faint and collapse to coma, because of false suspicions, cowardliness and anxieties.

As we learn through this topic, we should understand that Poverty is an obstacle to the manifestation of God's Glory in our lives. In order to sustain a glorious atmosphere in our entities, we ought to maintain our spiritual lives first, which carries by simply doing God's will and living according to His statutes. Then, that's when God's provision will be affirmed in our lives, as we lean on Him for sustainability. This edifies that living a better life reflects sincere expression of true worship, since worship is after Glory, yet better life elevates a Glorious living. In life, people live according to their different levels. For example, there are those of the first class, second and of the third. Even when it comes to recognition on several occasions, there are those of the cooperate class who receive a red carpet welcome, then the middle class, and lastly the commoners. Even when it comes to the sitting order, guests sit accordingly. And for that reason, people always do whatever it takes to conserve their classes in order to stay recognized in their companionships. If in the secular world people strive to preserve their classes in their comradeship, then there is a call for everyone who was created and called for the glory of the Lord to do whatever it takes in order to maintain worship as career in life. How can we maintain our lifestyle of worship? Sustaining our relationship with the Holy Spirit is the concrete surety for living a life without stain and apologies. At this point of view, we need to respond positively in order to maintain success in our lives, because it is not about us, but for Him we live and win in this World full of tests and trials.

DESIRE

Lifestyle is a desire.

Desire can be defined as a sense of longing, yearning, craving, needing and loving a person, an object or an outcome. Desire can also refer to a strong wish, passion, thirst or want for something. In reference to lifestyle, desire is a particular state of mind which can be reliable as in the sense of defining one's way of living. People's actions and reactions build upon their strong feelings, meaning, most of the decisions concerning how to carry on a daily living counts on how you strongly feel about yourself, how well you wish to benefit before carrying on any final alternate step.

Desires differ depending on uniquenesses and differences in people. This simply means that people with bad feelings can act ridiculously, as well as people with good attitude act wisely, due to their constructive state of mind. Therefore, if worship is a lifestyle which is determined by feelings, then desire is one thing amongst the few which edifies worship as a way of living.

Desire comes from relating much; spending much time, and being so close to something or somebody. The more closer you get to a person, the more you develop feelings for each other.

Most people fall in love with wrong people, the same applies with relating to poor behaviors. This simply results from offering much time, and also giving much attention to dirty stuff.

People get obsessed to things that take most of their time, and they finally mess up their lives, in the way that life seems useless without their dirty hobbies. For example; Eve desired for the forbidden fruit which led to man's crush.

Reuben desired for his father's concubine and ended up defiling his father's bed.

David desired for Beersheba Uriah's wife and he sinned against God.

Amnon developed lustful desires for his own sister Tamar, and he finally raped her.

Samson's foolish desires made his greatness demolish in a scrimp moment, as he finally lost his eyes because he lacked self-control for his false desires.

Desires are drivers but not controllers. Here we understand that we are the sole controllers of our lives but not desires. When cows and dogs get on heat, they run looking for the male, but with humans, it is a different case where self-control is highly required.

A lifestyle is decided by how best it moves someone's life amongst the variety of alternatives which are beaten up by ones perception of how to live accordingly. In this sense, worship should advance from being acknowledged as just purpose, but also as a desire.

Feelings determine so strongly on what, where, how, and when to act for one to receive satisfaction after his desires are finally fulfilled. This implies that if worship is not strongly felt, then it cannot be a lifestyle, as in the sense of one's choice of how to live his life accordingly. Desire must be the core foundation of falling in love with worship. After feeling so strongly wanting to act, then worship as an act finally results.

There are so many things that one would have desired for, but worship should be the priority amongst the many that are felt for.

There is no wisdom compared to desiring for worship. *PROVERBS 8:11; For wisdom is better than rubies. And all the things that one desires cannot be compared to her.* We simply have to recall that as we live our day to day life, righteousness is determined by our righteous desires. In that, if worship is an act of righteousness, then we ought to desire for it, desperately. *PROVERBS 11:23; The desires of the righteous are only good. But the expectations of the wicked are wrath.*

Desire should also be based on longing for his name, and always in remembrance of Him according to ISAIAH 26:8.

CHOICE

Lifestyle is a choice.

Choice is an act of selecting or making decision when faced with two or more possibilities. Choice is one of the most compelling things in life, which defines people's way of living their past, present and future. This simply refers that every decision a person makes in life will always reflect in his future whether good or bad.

In life, I have discovered that my heart is the sincerest friend I have ever had, yet the most superior deceiver in life is my own eyes. There are innumerable good and elegant things at sight, yet a few right ones. You should also understand that amongst uncountable wonderful friends you have, there are a few true ones. There are multifarious glittering fancy things which appear like real Gold and diamond, yet typically faked. In this orientation, we ought to think twice whenever we are seemingly faced with two or more opportunities.

Choice is the most sensitive part of our life journey. For example, choosing a husband from gentlemen; choosing a wife from women is not as simple as many take it to be. It takes spiritual detectors to discern truth from deception, just like money detectors to tell a fake dollar. As gold is tested by fire, God tests a heart to find a David, and in this respect, choice should not be taken for granted.

Choosing rightly is where most of us fail in life. For example, the children of Israel chose Saul in preference to God, and they initially ended up in total regret. Imagine how Esau sold his birthrights for a mere bread and stew of lentils. This was also the similar stall, as Jacob was given Leah instead of Rachael. Imagine Jacob failing to identify a girl he had dated for seven years. Samuel literally anointed Eliab instead of David. In this reference, you shouldn't be flashing at making decisions in the midst of your confusion, yet not be slow at certain significant urgent issues that need your emergency response. You shouldn't always delay, yet ought to be moderate at often times at the important decisions especially those concerning your destiny, irreversibly. For example, choosing the right courses of your education career; marital issues should not be the ones you take to be personal. In such crucial moments, you need to seek counsel from either two or more trusted parties who are well experienced in those areas.

The most failures in life are the selfish and arrogant people.

The disrespectful to the elderly, regarding them to be run out of constructive ideas, totally fail in life.

People who despise counsel and correction fail in life.

People with poor listening skills always miss on wisdom.

The uninspired, unexposed and the inexperienced people totally fail in life.

People who always consider themselves right and perfect fail in life.

The greedy, proud and primitive people end up as total failures.

According to Dr. John C. Maxwell, he noted that failures in life lack spiritual mentors and business models. This is very true, and for this case everyone who seeks for success in life should first seek for mentorship.

There was a certain young lady in a certain church, who fell in love with a Muslim man and sought counsel from her spiritual leaders who did not support her choice but advised her to drop the relationship and wait on God for the rightful partner of which she denied. This young lady, who was so much in love with the guy, just went straight to her lover and told him everything that was said by the pastor which opposed her love affair. The guy persuaded the girl not to go back to church, as she was also blinded by love agreed with him as well. There then she had no one to advise her any more, since she had disconnected herself from the church and had lost her way hopelessly.

After a period of time, as she knew that she was pregnant, she couldn't wait to surprise her fiancée with this interesting news, which obviously sounded like tidings of joy to him. Finally, this man proposed to her for an official marriage in his Muslim faith. After a period of one year in marriage, as she had even already given birth to a baby boy, this is when she discovers that her man had other three wives, even before she married him. This lady fainted as she imaged herself being the fourth wife, and after she had suffered so much, she comes back to the church regretting and crying "I was so stupid, I wish I waited upon God." At this time, it was already late to reverse her pastor's advice that seemed as nonsense in her hearing at the beginning. As a result of her breakdown, this girl eventually made up a decision, never to fall in love again due to the crush of her first marriage experience. Unfortunately, after a period of few years, she died of HIV infection.

There are so many people who live in misery and start putting blame on their parents, as to why they were born. They also curse their birthdays, yet it was their own fault in their poor decision making that made them end up in regret. Most of the messes we hit in life are neither our parents' faults, nor anybody else's responsibility, but we should accept to take the full blame upon ourselves, as we correct the mistakes of our past.

Parents try to do such a pivotal task of raising their children, after giving them an opportunity to come on this planet. As parents we play such an acute role of educating our children, but we can neither detect nor discern their destiny. It is always the wrong choices that all of us make, as we try to select one of the many possibilities which seem to be opportunities at our point of view. Most of our foolish prospects windup not according to our expectations, and result to a full blast regret in our entire life. This is possibly due to one's wrong perception of things, and finally poor decisions result.

This is also the same manner regarding to the wisdom of God. God has always given us the right over decision making, in order to choose which way to go in life. And in this case, the Lord will never stand in our way to hinder us from getting to our decided destined ends, whether good or bad. *DEUTRONOMY 11:26.Behold I set you this day a blessing and a curse. DEUTRONOMY 30:15. Behold I have set before you this day life and good, evil and death.* This alternately means that whenever a bad decision comes our way, there is always a way for escape by choosing the right thing. *REVELATION 3:8. Behold I have set before you an open door that no one can shut.* This scripture makes it clear that the right of decision making lies within you, and for that reason, I pray that you choose rightly.

Chapter 5

WORSHIP IS A WEAKNESS:

In this fifth chapter of our study, worship is interpreted as a weakness. Here a great mystery about God is revealed.

However, as weakness is misinterpreted in numerous ways, this commentary defines weakness in a series of clear interpretation.

Weakness is not wickedness. Implying, weakness is not a sin, errors and mistakes. A weakness is a weakling. It is a fragility, debility and feebleness for something, especially that particular thing you fill like you're meaningless without. A weakness is something that one lives for; something that brings meaning in a person's life; something that one cannot do without. A weakness can also be defined as a sense of loving, wanting and needing beyond control. Weakness is a sense of being over driven, over attracted, over obsessed, overwhelmed and overtaken by something beyond normal measures. A Weakness is a need or desire, a longing or wanting, beyond patience.

However, a weakness can either be constructive or destructive; positive or negative. Meaning, a weakness is neutral, depending on a person's state of mind.

Everyone has gotten a point of strength and of weakness at the same time, but the two are likely the same, meaning none of us can live without the two.

Despite the fact that God is the greatest and AL Powerful, God bears a sense of weakness as well. This is also the same nature which reflects in man, as a matter of fact that man is after God's own image.

 If God bears a weakness in Him, then what would that be? Which weakness is it that God cannot do or live without? If there is any weakness in God, there must not be any, other than worship! Indeed, God cannot do without worship. Worship is the fragility, debility and the feebleness in God. Worship is the seventh sense of God. It is what makes Him complete, thus God without worship is not God but an Idle. Worship is like God's utmost love, wanting and desire. Worship is the only sense which can attract, obsess and motivate God into action. Worship moves God emotionally. Worship touches God's heart, beyond prayers. Once you discover someone's priority and provide His most desire, you can simply win his heart, without fail.

Whenever we worship God, His Glory runs all over the Heavens, and also descends down to the Earth in the midst of His Holy Assemblies.

Every war strategist learns about the weakness of his opponent in order to come up with a superlative plan that can bring his enemy down. The chances of over powering your enemy rely on how much you know about his weakness.

Goliath was a champion in the Philistine arms, who were a common enemy of Israel. Goliath was a man of a fierce stature; the strong army of Israel fainted just at his appearance form of a giant whenever he showed out.

Goliath's height was six cubits and a span (9.75f, 2.9m). He had a bronze element on his head and a coat of mail which weighed 5000 shekels (57kg) of bronze, and a bronze armor on his legs and javelin between his shoulders. The staff of Goliath's spear was like a weavers beam, and his iron spearhead weighed 6000 shekels (6.8kg). As fierce and great Goliath was, nobody could believe that this champion could die like a raven with a mere stone by a little untrained field boy, David. Goliath's size and fierceness which was like a blast to the army of Israel, was instead an opportunity for David to win and prevail over him. David's victory relied much on Goliath's fierceness, whose size and height were so great to fight and win, yet his head was huge enough to escape the slung of the stone. In this legend, we learn quiet a big lesson, that most of the oversized problems and challenges that the devil brings our way are only huge in sight, but not in fight. We should understand that the devil's strongest weapon is fear. The enemy uses fierce figures and huge statures to make us faint even before the fight. For this reason, we should resist fear by faith, because faith is the only weapon which has the ability to defeat fear. And in this articulation, we should bear in mind that faith is the strongest weapon on Universe.

The accountability of Lucifer regarding to Worship
The love in God for worship is beyond apprehension, and due to His desire for worship he created the Angels to quench his thirst.

Amongst the Angels who were created, Lucifer was promoted, as the lead worshiper.

Lucifer simply means a bearer of light or morning star, and these refer to his former splendor as he was the greatest of all the Angels. Lucifer was highly anointed, and was adorned by God with such precious stones like the Sardius, toparz, and diamond, beryl, onyx, and jasper, sapphire, turquoise, and emerald with Gold. Lucifer was the lead worshiper in Heaven, and through his worship he ushered the rest of the heavenly hosts [angels] into God's presence. God made him as a seal of perfection. And He filled him with wisdom and perfect beauty. God also established him on His Holy mountain in order to offer Him the most opt praise and worship. EZEKIEL 28, ISAIAH 14:12-15.

Because of God's feebleness for worship, Lucifer was promoted as the captain over the Heavenly Angels.

Worship is God's prime wanting and desire; it is his feebleness and debility. And, since God was so much addicted to worship even to the point that He could not live without worship, this made Lucifer be God's priority since he held such a glorious gift as a worship leader. Eventually Lucifer became God's feebleness, debility and fragility to the extent that God could not do without him. But as time went on, Lucifer's heart was lifted in pride because of his beauty, wisdom and talents, and iniquity was found in him, as he became more violent and sinned within. He skimmed in his heart and thought that there is no way God could do without him. And as he falsely deemed in his heart that no one could perform better than he did, he developed such pride within his heart. Lucifer ended up rebellious even to the pick of leading a chaos in Heaven, and eventually a war broke out in Heaven, where he ended up a loser and also lost his position, together with a third of the Heavenly angels who collided with him in this revolt. Lucifer and his supporters were finally cast down-pit into the underworld, waiting for their final day of judgment. Lucifer was termed Satan, dragon and old serpent after his fall, as a result of him protesting against God.

As worshipers, we should learn from the Lucifer's fall, and we live a humble life without pride, considering ourselves for having been chosen by grace, but not by our own making.

When Angel Lucifer fell off the glory, man took over his position as a lead worshiper. Meaning, God has lifted man above the Angels, as the lead worshiper for his Glory. Here, we should understand that True and sincere worship is expressed by us the humans, and his Glory rises from here on Earth to heaven whenever we worship. And for this reason, it is clear enough to understand why Satan has such hatred towards humans, for having taken over his position as lead worshipers.

After worship had been affected by Lucifer's crush with the a third of the Heavenly angels, God the superior planer still came up with a superlative idea for the sake of his everlasting Glory through His worship.

GENESIS 1:26; Then God said, "let Us make man in our own image, according to our own likeness;

God created man to simply succeed and substitute the position of the fallen angels, and also to redeem and reestablish His darling worship. Implying, worship is the purpose for creation.
For worship we were created, and for this new project God formed man. Here we should understand that God has assigned us for this purpose, and while we live in this world, we are here for training which transforms us into better people for this internal purpose. In this case, we ought to lecture on true worship, in order to qualify and worship Him for eternity.
The Lord tests us through this mortal life of our Earthly familiarity, as he watches how we worship Him the invisible one in faith. Meaning, if we can love, trust and believe the supernatural one and also worship Him, the unseen God, then we qualify to see His face and live in His everlasting glorious presence for eternity.

God created Adam and Eve and based them in the Garden of Eden to represent us all in the test of obedience. This definitely means that when the first Adam fell at the Genesis, we all fell in him. But, when the second Adam overcame the Earth, we got our victory through Him. And for this reason, we can still come to the Father through our Lord Jesus Christ, without fear.

FAITH IS TESTED

There was a certain Christian organization, which owned single sex schools, one for girls and another school for boys. An idea of turning these single schools into a one mixed school came up one day, and before their vision was established, it was tested by mixing two girls from the single girl's school with the boys for a period of a year to represent the rest of the girls. Unfortunately, at the end of the year as it was the period given for the tryout, these two girls were examined and both were found pregnant, and the whole idea failed due to the negative results from the assessment.

As it is well-known that samples are always taken from amongst the best, Adam and Eve were better than all of us. And in this clarification, even if it were you and me to represent the rest of the world in this examination in the Garden of Eden, we would obvious act the same way that Adam and Eve did. In this sense, we should not put our blame on Adam and Eve for having failed the test. And we should understand that even though we failed in Adam, still God came up with a new strategy through Jesus Christ, who brought us back into reconciliation with the Father.

At this point of view, as we consider worship being a weakness in God, we should apprehend that God cannot live without us, as we learn through this version that we have been preferred by God to bring about his Glory through our worship. And since weakness is about loving, wanting, longing and dying for something or person, here we acknowledge that we are God's most extreme weakness. God is so much addicted to us. We are His utmost love and want. Meaning, we are his maximum feebleness, debility and fragility, and for this reason, God cannot do without us.

Considering the fact that we love God and have now discovered His weakness, we should always worship for Him to count on us, as we count on him for our weaknesses as well.

We should not take worship lightly, but as something very darling to God. We minister to people through preaching and teaching, but we can only minister to God through our worship. And for this reason, we should consider worship as the core of our church services.

In church today, as we carry out many programs like testimonies, teachings, fundraisings, Holy Communion, prayer and intercessions, we are the key beneficiaries but not God. Therefore, we ought to offer God, crème de la crème, worship, as the best that we can offer for His everlasting Glory.
All the activities carried in church are relevant, but worship is the focal goal that we should not oversight. As we preach, teach and pray harder, should be the similar manner in learning how well we can truly worship and please God.

Worship is the song, tune and fragrance of God's presence.
In this apprehension, we should grasp that all the activities carried out in church are simply to prepare a worshiper's heart.

Chapter 6

WORSHIP IS NOT MUSIC

PSALMS 150:1-5 1 Praise the LORD. Praise God in his sanctuary; praise him in his mighty heavens. 2 Praise him for his acts of power; praise him for his surpassing greatness. 3 Praise him with the sounding of the trumpet, praise him with the harp and lyre, 4 praise him with timbrel and dancing, praise him with the strings and pipe, 5 praise him with the clash of cymbals, praise him with resounding cymbals.

Music is the art of sound in time that expresses ideas and emotions, in significant forms through the elements of rhythm, melody, harmony, and color. Music can also be defined as a vocal or instrumental sound (or both), combined in such a way as to produce the beauty of harmony, and expression of emotions.

David was one of the greatest kings of Israel. His variant deeds were recorded and will always be read about and also remembered. He is recalled as the second King over Israel, who fought and won many battles for his people. During his reign, he focused much on enlarging the territories of his Kingdom, of which he did with enormous success. On top of that, David was also a fabulous talented musician, and a skillful player of harps, which he played and demons fled. Besides that, David was also a tremendous song writer. He wrote seventy three Psalms with the most famous one; "PSALMS 23; "The Lord is my shepherd." These Psalms were songs composed by David, and other writers like the sons of Korah, Asaph, Heman, Ethan, Solomon, Moses, Haggai, Zechariah and Ezra.

Imagine a kind of worship, were kings and rulers are the lead soloists and harpists. Imagine a kind of worship, were even demons cannot withhold. King David lived a life of a true worshiper. He worshiped God through his talent in music. Humble worshipers like David are not common in the present era. Many people take the music ministry in church as the least of all, and also as for the spiritual amateurs and young people who have not yet discovered their areas of gifting. There are few churches where pastors live as role models to their followers regarding to worship through music.

Many church leaders dodge the worship session and spend most of their time in their offices during worship. Most preachers don't participate in worship services, as they take the message they preach to be more important than this purpose for life. We should note that we minister to God through worship, and God also ministers to us through the word.

Solomon the wisest King ever lived spoke three thousand proverbs of wisdom. But, on top of that he expressed his wisdom through music rhythms and harmony. King Solomon wrote one thousand and five songs. Imagine the wisest King ever lived having expressed his wisdom through music! And we, as poor and least as we are to take music so lightly. Some of us don't worship God as we ought to, as most people view worship as an entertainment session, and at this occasion people pace around, and others think of easing themselves, as they wrongly think that the most important session is prayer and listening to the word, so they view worship as a break or an entertainment session. I have watched people moving up and down during the praise and worship session, without knowledge that worship is the crème of our church services. This is the session when the all universe is on alert, as the angels and twenty four elders lay down, and every creature bows to worship before the throne of God.

When time for worship arrives, every activity in Heaven stops, as the angels worship God along with us. Worship is an act of faith, which brings Glory to God as expressed out of love and gratitude for who He is! You cannot separate worship from music, because harmonies and rhythms express one's feelings and emotions acutely, even beyond other forms of worship. Meaning, music is the best expression of worship amongst them all. However, the difference between music and worship is that in music art of sound is very important as a clear expression, yet in worship faith is the center of our expression. Even though emotions are what we share in common for both worship and music, the uniqueness about the two is the definite deviation in the ideas behind both animations.

WORSHIP IS NOT MUSIC but MUSIC CAN BE WORSHIP.

Worship is not music, but music can be worship. In this reverence, we understand that if worship was music, then the non-talented would have not been created. Man is a product of worship. When God created man, He made us in his alikeness but with uniqueness in aptitude, ability and capacity. Each one of us was created with a unique gift, and this was purposed for us to offer worship in magnificently different fashions through our modifications as in different styles of expressions like music.

Worship is not music but music can be worship. This is because music is after art of sound, rhythm or harmony that expresses one's emotions. Emotions being the lead expression of one's idea behind the vim of worship, this makes music fitting for worship. In this coordination, there is no a better way of expressing emotions than music. For there is a way rhythms move one's spirit, as the heart also boosts to release the utmost expression compared to other forms of worship. For example; when someone feels a song, the all body responds by dancing, as the hands also re-join by clapping, and in most cases you find yourself sobbing. Truly, there is no a person who can resist the rhythm of music, whether talented or non-talented. However, we should apprehend that music can only be meaningful depending on which message communicated in the art of the sound. And as we rely on music as the best form of our expression in this bid of worship, the message should always take the lead, along with the rhythm as the accompaniment. In this manner, we ought to be focused as we do our worship through music, in pursuance of not losing the sensibility and sincerity of our countenance. And by acting in this manner, our singing and accompaniment will gain significance to God. There are so many worshipers as in the modern church setting, who only mind at their vocals and instrumentals and miss on the denotation of the act. Most of the time we focus on how we sound to listeners around, and we forget about the interest of the one we ought to please. God is not after art, though it is also important to be organized as in the sense of presentation for the sweetness of our act. God's utmost joy is when we earnestly mean what we say, right from within.

One day I visited a certain church in a worship service, where I noticed that people's emotions were being rolled over by the accompaniments but not their sincere cognizance. Unfortunately, as worship was still carrying on, power went off, and the accompaniments also stopped as well. Then all of a sudden, the feeling of the song and people's emotions also changed instantly, as if it was the machines which were the lead, and the choir was just backing-up the accompaniments. And as I looked at the choir which was leading the congregation to the throne room, they were all looking at each other as if the songs that they were singing were mere mimes not real live presentations. In the realm of worship, we should note that machines are just accompaniments, but they don't accurately meet God's neediness for worship.

Worship is done by We the living, since we bare the quality of true worshipers; body, mind and Spirit.

PSALMS 150:6. Let everything that has breath praise the Lord.

This scripture is like an awakening call that breath is the password for worship. This edifies that we should rely much on ourselves than machines, because machines have no emotions as we do, yet God's is interest is in the way we feel as we worship.

God is not like man to be moved just by the beats of musical instruments, He is after a worshiper's heart. And since a worshiper has lived before the accompaniments, yet the focal reason for our existence is worship, God is after the sincerity behind the emotions of a worshiper but not instrumentals. And, if worship was after accompaniments, then man would have not been born naked! Man would have been born well dressed in a choir uniform, holding a quitter to confirm that true worship is after accompaniments. In this sense, we acknowledge that machines are man-made to accompany us on this occasion. Therefore, we should always rehearse on how to worship God with or without accompaniments for his peculiar Glory.

We should consider this in mind that manmade musical instruments are not the center of our worship. Therefore, we should never be replaced by any other artificial element on this purpose. One of the most important points that we should not miss on is that worship is a purpose but not an entertainment business. In this sense, we should not be paid money for this progression. God has already invested in us all His beauty at the creation. We are God's concrete property; we belong to Him; we are His own for this purpose, and He has already invested in us to profit Him. As God breathed in us a breath of life at the creation, He provided everything in us at the beginning, and there is totally nothing that we lack to hinder our worship. God invested in us the beautiful world that we live in; the beautiful weather changes beyond description, together with the beauty in the space; the Sun, the Moon and the Stars in the sky; the clouds in the beautiful blue sky, for there is totally nothing which was made imperfect to hinder our sincere worship. Therefore, we should not hire anybody at any cost for this sequence of worship, whether instrumentalists or trainers. Everyone should serve in church willingly, with awareness that we don't worship God for anything else, but purpose is the bid behind every contribution of our distinctive talents in church.

Chapter 7

WORSHIP IS NOT UTTERANCE

REVELATION; 4:8 "Holy, holy, holy, Lord God Almighty, Who was and is and is to come!

Worship is the only act of faith beyond words and natural understanding. The supremacy, beauty and awesomeness of the AL mighty God are beyond description. There are utterly no words which can refer to the beauty of His dwelling place, the Heavens. The beauty of Heaven is inexpressible. There are no words in the natural to describe the realism of Heaven. If the Heavens bare such an indescribable beauty, how exceeding is the beauty of the creator of all, the beyond compare heavenly atmosphere.

REVELATION4:8; the four living creatures, each has six wings, were full of eyes around and within. And they do not rest day and night, saying; "Holy, Holy, Holy, Lord God Almighty, who was and He is and He is to come.

Worship is far beyond utterance, meaning, there's no expertise in this deed. Most people compose and rehearse multifarious words to practice in there worship, as they think that God's heart is merely moved by numerous lyrics. In this acquaintance we absorb that God's worthiness, awesomeness, greatness, beauty, glory, power, honor and supremacy is unutterable and unbelievable, and this is the reason as to why the four living creatures for days and nights never cease to utter repeatedly; Holy, Holy, and holy, are you Lord God Almighty. Those seemingly to be fewer words in utterance, mean a lot to God. Therefore, we should not equate God with humans who live by deception and manipulate our God with what seem to sound fragrant in our hearing. The seemingly to be littler words like; Hosanna, Glory, Worthy and Halleluiah; is the utmost praise and worship, beyond compare. We should also note that it is only and only God who is acknowledged with such exaltations.

Worship is not mere words, but more of honor and reference to God.

ISAIAH 6:2; above it stood Seraphim; each one had six wings: with two he covered his face, with two he covered his feet, and with two he flew.

God is the glorious brightest light, his face shines a trillion times brighter than the sun, and no eyes can barely look at his face. For this reason, the Seraphim therefore cover up their eyes, and they cover their feet in reference to God's Holy presence. We ought to learn that as worshipers our expression should be presented in a very honorable and respectful way in reference to God's peculiar Glory. We should understand that by honoring God is the utmost worship beyond words.

REVELATION 4: 10; the twenty-four elders fall down before Him who sit on the throne and worship Him who lives forever and ever, and cast their crowns before the throne.

In this scripture we grasp that worship is humbleness, self-denial and total brokenness before God's awesome presence. And as we cast down our crowns, honor and dignity, and exalt Him above the universe, there's nothing compares to worship with full expression. We ought to worship with full expression of our deeper feeling. This doesn't necessarily mean that whatever expression that we show on the outside is the real feeling within. A person can possibly play the opposite of his real feelings, because feelings are a heartfelt sequence. In the spiritual realm, hearts speak louder than the physical utterance, meaning there's nothing hidden from God. Therefore, at the bid of worship, God considers a heart than utterances.

As humans judge according to the natural sight and intellect, God's point of view is far beyond natural standards. God searches the depth of heart, this is where every mystery and secrets are revealed and left uncovered. In this reflection, there is absolutely nothing that is hidden from God's sight. Men can hide their true personalities with fellow men, manipulate each other, but God knows everything and He is always ahead of time.

PROVERBS 14:5; A faithful witness will not tell lie but a false witness will utter lies.

People witness by utterance, of which most false witnesses take it as an opportunity to falsely accuse others with false claims. And for this reason, detecting truth from deception sometimes becomes trying and challenging, since truth dwells in heart where man can hardly access but only God. For this reason, God does not dance by the tune of multifarious words, God searches the heart.

JAMES 3:8; "But no human being can tame the tongue it is a restless evil, full of deadly poison", the tongue can be the most wicked weapon on the Earth.

This scripture clarifies how wicked the tongue is. Therefore, our worship should not rely on spoken words, but should be an act of in-depth sensation. God is not overawed by the harmony of mere words, since most of us are good at smooth-talking and persuading. God's prime interest is in the uprightness of a worshiper's heart than a manipulative tongue of a decent speaker. We ought to speak love which over flows right from within. We should always speak of His goodness with deeper feeling, but not like a poem. At this point of view, we should acknowledge that the heart speaks louder than the electronic power addressing systems to God.

Chapter 8

WORSHIP IS HEART

1 SAMUEL 16:7; but the Lord said to Samuel, "Do not look at his appearance or at his physical stature, because I have refused him. For the Lord does not see as man sees; for man looks at the out ward appearance, but the Lord looks at the heart.

You're a person but not a personality. Your true entity is not defined by your fine-looking appearance, behaviors, character and words. Rather, your heart edifies the real you. Meaning, you're heart. Personalities can be adopted from a person you admire; behaviors can be learned from your peers; character develops with time, but a heart is too original to be duplicated, faked and imitated.

Your heart is your mind, master-planner, decision maker, store-safe, and your number one asset. Everything you experience in life revolves around your heart as the driver; that is to say your heart is the Centre of dreams, desires and decisions. Your heart is a store-safe. Money is kept in banks, goods in ware houses, food in refrigerators, but wisdom, ideas, dreams, visions and secrets are safer in heart. Your heart is your number one asset; it is your greatest wealth; your heart is bigger than the world and with it you can own the entire world and possess wealth. Your heart is a treasury. Everything that seems to be important to you is kept at heart. In this case, we should guard our hearts as our own lives. And in this manner, we should not entrust people with our hearts, because there is totally nothing that treasures and values to heart, on this universe.

You should always own 100% shares of your heart, because no one can value your feelings, desires and emotions the way you do. You can never share your heart with anybody, just like your five senses can't be shared with your family, partners and lovers. Most of the times people share with me what they go through, and I also respond like "I know how you feel" yet the mere fact; I can't feel someone else's brunt of the pain. There was a certain man, who had a bag full of notes of over a million dollars. This man met a friend ridding back home, and asked him to keep his bag for a night in fear of being attacked and robbed by thieves at his home in the night. The gentle man who was given the task of the bag without awareness of what the bag really carried didn't even bother to check it and store it in a safer place. This man just left the bag in his car boot. The next morning, as he took the car for washing, a boy who was cleaning the car discovered the money in the bag and disappeared with it. Then that very morning, the owner of the bag gets to his friend to have his luggage, and this man gets into his car to bring the bag and finds that the bag had already been stolen. The owner of the bag screamed in tears like "What have you done to me; am finished" his friend also responded, as he promised to buy him a new bag with everything he had lost within the stolen bag, without knowledge of what exactly had been lost in the bag. And then the owner also responded like "even if you give your own life, you cannot pay me back". And as the friend asked, and discovered what the stolen bag was carrying, they both carried together, yet nothing could be recovered, as the bag was already gone. In this story, pure wisdom and awareness is being communicated. You should not be deceived to entrust your heart with anybody. Because you are the only person who understands you, you should always love, care, trust and protect yourself better than anyone you love and care about. Your heart is like a piece of a delicate diamond. Most of the broken hearts break by the hands of trusties but not the true owners. Meaning, you can never disappoint you, whether you are right or wrong. We should also note that no one can mishandle your heart unless you give him a chance. Therefore, it is better we entrust our hearts only with our maker, who can bind and even mold us again whenever we breakdown. Your heart is a weapon for war; victory and defeat lays either at the braveness or the fragility of a warrior's heart. Meaning, determination is not masculinity but heart. David was small in size but yet a giant in heart that is why he was able to kill Goliath. Your heart is a business strategist; success and failure is determined by the state of your heart.

There are checkpoints at almost every public place entrance like banks, hotels, hospitals, shopping malls and at Air fields. At every security point, people and objects go through detecting machines, as one of the measures to ensure safety for lives of people in public places. In these security systems, there is totally nothing like harms and drugs which can go through undetected. But, a heart is the only thing which passes through security systems untouched, whether dangerous or not. Your heart is the master controller of your life; once a heart is won, the entire body has no choice but to obey.

Nebuchadnezzar was a great king in the ancient days of Babylon. God had made him King over kings in his days. The God of Heavens had given him Kingdom, power, strength and glory. Wherever the children of men dwelt, the beasts of the sea and the birds of the air, God had given into his hands and He ruled over every being. Nebo is a Chaldean word meaning God. Nebuchadnezzar was a god to the Chaldeans. In his magnitude, he killed whomever he hated, and according to his word, he let anyone live as he willed. But when God determined to humble Nebuchadnezzar, he turned his heart into a beast's heart. And one day, as King Nebuchadnezzar walked around his royal palace of Babylon, something happened to him, and he transformed into a typical beast in understanding and conduct. As his mind changed into a beast, he could no longer behave as humans do. A man, who was highly honored, started moving out of his chambers naked, crawling like an animal with both legs and arms. Imagine a man, who used to have fine meals at the king's table, starting eating grass like an oxen. He could no longer sit on his throne as a king, but jumping around his chambers as an animal. He could neither speak, nor reason like he used to, but only scream like a fox.

Imagine, how the nobles of the kingdom consulted from almost every magician, doctors and wizards in order to diagnose his illness, and still there was no solution for his condition. His disorder gave a very hard-time to his maidens and attendants, as they had to force their king to have bath and also make him dress-up. It was quiet a testing moment for his wives and siblings, as they watched their royalty and the great kingdom demolishing with no one to help.

His royal guards tried much as they could to seize him on chains for the situation not to go beyond the palace, but still he broke them off and escaped until the news spread all over the world that the great King had turned into a beast. As the situation worsened beyond control, they finally let him join his fellows in the jungle. He lived at the fields and his body was wet with the dew of heaven, till his hair grew like eagles' feathers, and his nails like birds' claws. Seven seasons passed over him; until he knew that the Most High rules in the kingdom of men, and gives it to whomever he chooses. After the end of seven seasons, Nebuchadnezzar regained back his rightful mind and senses, and a man who had lived his passed as a god to the Chaldeans, finally turned into a worshiper. Imagine, a man like Nebuchadnezzar, praising God with such powerful exaltations;

"I praise the most high and honor him who lives forever. For His dominion is an everlasting dominion.

And His kingdom is from generations to generations. All the inhabitants of the Earth are reputed as nothing. He does according to his will in the army of Heaven. And among the inhabitants of the Earth no one can restrain his hand or say to Him," what have you done?"

It takes God's hand for a proud king like Nebuchadnezzar to be humbled and turn into a worshiper for Jehovah God of the Universe with search exaltations. Surely, God holds the hearts of the kings in his hands, and turns them wherever he wants.

PROVERBS 21:1The king's heart is in the hands of the Lord, like the rivers of water; he turns it wherever He wishes.

And in this manner, we learn that God touches a heart to transform a person. Once God touches a heart, things just change automatically; your heart is the remote controller of your life. And of all the parts of your body, God desires your heart the most. In worship, your heart is the sole lead, as the rest of your body obeys. Heart is the Centre of life; it control ones desires, feelings, choices, attitude, towards action or reaction based on the battle of decision within.

WORSHIP IS GOD"S HEART.

Worship is God's heart. Worship is the Centre of God's love, will, purpose and desire. It is solely worship which strongly touches God's heart and also charges the capability of His supremacy for manifestation.

Since worship is God's heart, we should note that as worshipers we bear God's premier desire and will. Meaning, whenever we worship as we ought to, we can easily win God's heart, that is to say, His love, desire and will are finally affirmed in our lives. Heart being the controller of life, worship controls God and the entire Heaven. True worship makes God moved, and sometimes he can even cry just at the sweetness and the vim of worship arising from the Earth. God cannot resist worship. It is solely at worship that God loses control over willpower. As life revolves around heart, Godliness also revolves around worship. It is only and solitarily at worship that God gets on tiptop. Worship is God's dancing tune. With worship, you can control God's attention. Worship is life to God. Worship is God's heartbeat. Worship is like a hobby and an addiction to God, for He cannot do without worship!

Chapter 9

WORSHIP

IS

GIVING

ACTS 20:35;
And remember the words of the Lord Jesus, that He said, „it is more blessed to give than to receive."

Giving is the utmost worship, beyond words. Giving speaks louder than verbal expression. Show me a true worshiper, and I will tell by the level of His or her giving! True worship is all about giving. Givers demonstrate sincere worship, beyond compare. God is so much moved by a mere giving than serious prayers. Meaning, God is overawed by actions than words.
ACTS 10:31; Cornelius; your prayer has been heard, and your giving to the poor has reached Heaven.

A gift is an expression of true worship. A gift expresses sincere worship and love, beyond words.

MATHEW 2:11 And when they had come into the house, they saw the young child with Mary His mother, and fell down and worshiped Him, and when they had opened their treasures they presented gifts to Him: Gold, Frank incense, and Myrrh.

In here, we learn that giving is part of our worship. And as we clearly examine this act of the wise men, after they had realized that a great King had been born, their motive for worship was accompanied by gifts. They carried gifts along with them, as they wisely knew that worship is not only a verbal expression, but it's all about giving. These amazing men backed their worship with gifts of gold and silver, as they worshiped the baby King with their gifts. Complete worship is giving, and giving

is the wisest deed for genuine worship .In this respect;
it takes a spirit of wisdom for someone to worship with
a gift.

WORSHIP IS AN OFFERING.

*PROVERBS 3:9; Honor the Lord with your possessions
and with the first produce of your entire increase.*

Giving is the ultimate worship, beyond words. In this
respect, as we learn to worship our God with our
material possessions, we should understand that an
offering is a fruit of faith. Worship is not all about vibe,
it is about a gift. As worshipers, we should absorb that
true worship goes beyond lyrics, to being a test, thus a
turn of faith. True worship is tested and examined by a
genuine and cheerful giving. Giving material
possessions and the first fruits of our produces is the true
expression of our living faith since faith without action
is dead. Giving is the affirmation of our faith behind our
sincere expression of worship. Giving plays quite a big
role in expressing and affirming complete worship.
Worship without giving is like eating a half-baked cake.

This lesson can be well guided by the following
questions:-
How often do you listen to messages about giving?
How do you feel about giving?

What is your motive towards giving?
Are you a giver?
Do you feel hard-time about giving?
Have you ever given your best?

Being that worship is giving, let's pose the question in the angles of worship.
Whatever message that is preached about giving is all about worship.
The way you feel about giving is your feeling towards worship
Your motive towards giving is your sincere mind towards worship
You cannot be a worshiper if you are not a giver

Feeling hardship at giving is feeling hardship at worship

Giving your best is the best worship you can ever give.

Some preachers hardly teach about giving than they teach about worship with a negative view over this deed. Some church leaders fear to preach the truth of this knowledge about the principle of giving. Most of the young preachers criticize this truth, as many of them take it to be a manipulative kind of preaching. Giving money is a Godly principle, for the well-establishment and the daily running of the church body. However, there are some false preachers who have abused this truth for their personal gains. Giving is one of the five preeminent pillars of the church and a superlative form of worship.

We should also understand that money is not the only gift that expresses giving as a form of worship. We should understand that everything we own can be given to God as a form of worship. Therefore, as we offer our lives; bodies, spirits, and mind, and as we offer our time, blessing, glory and honor to God, it is the sincerest transcendent worship that we can ever give to God.

Giving is a blessing.
Givers are the most successful people in life, well as receivers always live without enough. Worship is not only expressed in music and utterance, but even more practical in Giving. If worship is heart and yet heart is the controller of even the material wealth, then there should not be anything reserved for selfish ambitions as we present our sincerity to God. This simply elevates that wherever one's wealth is, so will the heart and mind also be.

MATEHEW 6:21 "for where your treasure is, there your heart will be also.

Multifarious songs that we sing only speak about offering hearts to God, yet we resist at offering our money to Him. I always wonder, of the two; meaning the heart and money, which is the most valuable? I have noticed that most people value money in reference to their hearts. However, here we learn that we shouldn't offer what we value less.

GIVING IS A TEST.

God views our giving as a trying moment. And since a man's heart dwells in his treasury, God also love it the way He tests our worship, love and faithfulness through these material possessions. In that, we cannot give hearts and be hesitant at giving money to God. How often have you been timid at giving, but fast at verbal expression? Resistance at giving is like striking an own goal. In this acknowledgement, we should understand that we are the main beneficiaries of our own giving but not God.

OFFERING ACCEPTABLE

GENESIS 4: 4, 5 4; Abel also brought of the first born of his flock and of their fat. And the Lord respected Abel and his offering. 5; But did not respect Cain and his offering.

Which lesson do we learn from the text? In here, we learn that worship as an offering is not just a matter of any gift, but the quality also matters adequately. An offering is something which is offered as a gift or contribution for someone to accept or reject. In this manner, we should always choose the best of our vintages in order to be acceptable. Acceptance relies much on the quality of the gift offered. God can either accept or reject any of our worship. Respect is also pointed out in this scripture. As we worship God with our offering, He can either respect or disrespect us with our gifts, accordingly. Therefore, we ought to know that you cannot respect someone who is not important to you. Meaning, whenever we act as expected in regard to worship, then that's when we bare significance to the Lord. It is also very vivid that an offering speaks louder and better than a persuasive tongue. Giving digs deeper into God's heart than any other forms of worship that we can ever give!

GIVING EDIFIES TRUE LOVE.

Love without giving is insincere. For this reason, if worship is a gift of love to God, then the expression has to be accompanied with gifts. Love without sharing is false. Giving is alternatively the best way for expressing true worship by the untalented in singing, dancing and many other ways that require special talents and skills. People with disabilities like the lame, blind, the dame and mute, may be left out in music as a form of worship if giving has not been emphasized in particular. People with disabilities also love the Lord, though they can't express their gratitude in the same way others who physically function well do. This shouldn't be an excuse for them to escape the truth of complete worship. They should also give the little that they can afford, cheerfully. Giving should be specifically identified as the most decent form of worship, which does not require someone to participate in singing, dancing and gestures. Action speaks louder and also better than verbal expression.

*JOHN 3:16. "For God so loved the world and He gave his only begotten son that who so ever believes in Him shall not die but have an everlasting life".*This simply means that it is not just verbal, but true love is all about giving. We cannot love God by mere words. We should also share gifts with Him since love is about sharing. We must learn to test God with our offering in order to give Him room for action. We should understand that whenever we hesitate on giving we automatically limit God's manifestation in our lives.

MALACHI 3:4 Then the offering of Jerusalem and Judah would be pleasant to the Lord. 5; And I will come near you for judgment. I will be a swift witness against; the sorcerers, the adulterers, the perjurers, and against those who exploit wage earners and widows and orphans. EXODUS 10:24, 25, 26 Then pharaoh said to Moses and said "Go, serve the Lord; only let your flocks and birds be kept back, let your little ones go with you".

25-But Moses said, "you must also give us sacrifices and burnt offerings, that we may sacrifice to the Lord our God. 26-Our livestock shall also go with us; not a hoof shall be left behind. For we must take some of them to serve the lord our God, and even we do not know with what we must serve the Lord until we arrive there".

In case Pharaoh let them go and still held back their flocks, it would signify a meaningless journey because Israel cannot worship without offering. Here we note that every offering means much to God.

Chapter 10

TRUE WORSHIPER

John 4:23; yet a time is coming, and the hour is now, when the true worshiper will worship the Father in the spirit and truth, for the Father is seeking such a people.

What is truth? Truth comes from the word true. Truth is one thing, or even one of the few, which are not easy to define. However, truth can be simply defined as the sense of genuineness, factualness, exactness and rightness. Truth can also be described as the quality of being true. Truth is pointed out at many different biblical occasions, but it is not clearly defined as in any scriptural context. However, Jesus speaks of Himself as the truth, but not just true. In that, He exceeded from the level of just being true, and he became truth, Himself. *JOHN 14:6; Jesus answered, I am the way the truth and the life.* In here, Jesus demonstrates three things that He simply represents. But as we go through this chapter, Truth is our focal goal. Jesus referring Himself to truth and yet God's interest is in truth, it is the concrete clarification that Jesus the word and the very truth that we believe is the priority to God. Therefore, we should understand that except through God's only son our Lord Jesus Christ, there is no any other truth. And for this evidence, we accepting Him, whom He sent to us as the only way to the father, is the most significant lifetime decision. Jesus being the mediator who intercedes for us before the Father, we should know that once we have Him, then truth will also abide in us. Truth in regard to worship is well clarified with an enlightened scriptural backup. *John 4:23; yet a time is coming, and the hour is now, when the true worshiper will worship the Father in the spirit and truth, for the Father is seeking such a people.* In here, we see Jesus trying to relate truth with worship, as he pointed out God's desperate need for a true worshiper. In this conversation between Jesus and a Samaritan woman, there is a drive that literally takes both of them to the topic of worship. And here we learn that the stellar purpose for our creation was to worship, thus we are the center of worship. It is also very fundamental, for us to recognize that we ought to bear the qualities of true worshipers that are desirable of God. As a church, we should understand the mystery in this wisdom of God behind the scripture; *"yet a time is coming when true worshipers will worship the Father in spirit and truth"*. Man being three in one, that is to say body, spirit and mind, it is what brings an absolute meaning for the physical expression to be practical as an affirmation for real worship. And in this manner, we have to be aware that time always come, when the body separates from the spirit and mind, and the body gets back to the ground from which it was formed, and then the spirit and mind also return to their maker for their final judgment. At this spot of time, as the spirit and mind are separated from the body, this is when the spirit proves its true worship, without the physical nature of expression. This means that time will come when one will be separated from the two, meaning the body will be separated from the spirit and mind, and there the spirit and mind will live on their own without their body any more. This edifies that even though the three are associates in the physical expression of our worship, time will come when the form of worship will also change accordingly, as they no longer live in unison when one is dead, and we shall have to worship the father in spirit alone without our physical expression. The form of worship changes due to the fact that the spiritual expression of worship diversify the physical idea and perspective of worship. Our physical nature is much affected by the challenges that we face in life, and also driven by needs, desires and choices, which is the reverse to spirits. The Spirit doesn't bank on the physical drivers of life. For this reason therefore, true worship is offered by a spirit. Our spirits are the true worshipers that God is in hunt for. Spirits worship God for who He is. Spirits speak the truth. Relying on this fact that our spirits don't ride by the physical desires, our worship don't rely on God's performance, neither is it charged by God's works. Meaning, we worship God not because of what He has done, but because of who He is; with no personal gains or interests as to be expected in return. And in this sense, we learn that there is no manipulation in the spiritual worship, for it is sincere and true.

QUALITIES OF A SPIRITUAL WORSHIPER
- ➤ They are friends to the Holy Spirit.
- ➤ Their spiritual senses are always active.
- ➤ Their decisions are always discerned by the Spirit.
- ➤ They always under look the physical, and focused at the spiritual.
- ➤ They always think beyond the natural charisma.
- ➤ Their priorities are beyond man standards.
- ➤ They are patient and love waiting on the Lord.
- ➤ They are not greedy.
- ➤ They take God first.
- ➤ They are obedient to the Holy Spirit.
- ➤ They don't mind what others think or say, as long as they follow the instructions of the Holy Spirit.
- ➤ They do not live according to fleshly desires.
- ➤ They do not rely on their own strength and understanding.
- ➤ They are humble and calm in their spirits.
- ➤ They bear spiritual fruits.

NON-SPIRITUAL WORSHIPERS
- ➤ They are driven by their fleshly desires.
- ➤ They under look the spiritual and awed by the physical.
- ➤ They prefer natural standards to super natural standards.
- ➤ They are impatient, they want instant blessings.

- ➢ They are friendly to the worldly setting.
- ➢ Their spiritual senses are dormant.
- ➢ They lack a Spirit of discernment.
- ➢ They are greedy.
- ➢ They take God last.
- ➢ They are disobedient to the Holy Spirit.
- ➢ They live according to the flesh.
- ➢ They rely on their own strength.
- ➢ They are proud.
- ➢ They are fruitless and barren.
- ➢ They hate rebuke and correction.
- ➢ They live by sight not by faith.
- ➢ They are prayerful but disobedient.
- ➢ They pray for physical desires.

OTHER TITLES
By
Emmanuel Christoe